(continued from front flap)

was if you were red." The system *must* be mad, he says, if he was told in high school (1) Douglas MacArthur was the greatest American of the twentieth century, (2) the Nazis weren't all bad, after all some of Hitler's own generals tried to kill him, (3) the black slaves in the South had it fairly good until Reconstruction, when their troubles began, (4) the Industrial Revolution started because Robert Fulton as a child watched his mother make tea and applied the principles of the tea pot to designing the steam engine.

"Although it may seem I exaggerate," he says, "it is the truth, I swear, as God Himsel[f] still alive." D[...] cerned, Micha[el...] generation is m[ore...] than a history, infused with the author's keen sense of America's absurdity.

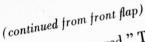

These are the good old days

Michael Myerson

These
are
the
good
old
days

Coming of age
as a radical
in America's
late, late years ☆

GROSSMAN PUBLISHERS, NEW YORK, 1970

This book is for
My Parents, first, without whom, etc.;
Lincoln, Jimmy and Zia Celine,
David and Sammy, from whom I'm learning now;
And for the brothers & sisters of Vietnam,
who show us the way.

Nora: "Those were the good old days."
Nick: "No, these are the good old days."
                    Dialogue from The Thin Man

He not busy being born is busy dying.
                                        BOB DYLAN

"Yossarian, we live in a age of distrust and
deteriorating spiritual values. It's a
terrible thing," Doc Daneeka protested in
a voice quavering with strong emotion.
"It's a terrible thing when even the word
of a licensed physician is suspected by the
country he loves."
                    JOSEPH HELLER, Catch-22

If you leave it to them, they will crochet
the world the color of goose shit.
                                    JACQUES BREL

Foreword

Ah, but I was so much older then
I'm younger than that now.

  BOB DYLAN

I remember, in June 1960, my older brother coming to visit me in San Francisco. For the past year and a half I had been a premature New Leftist, together with a relative handful of comrades. We had organized at Berkeley the only student political party in the country, and in 1959, already had a micro-free-speech movement which had resulted in two dozen of us receiving "disciplinary action." The spring just past had seen our work culminate in demonstrations to save Chessman, the Woolworth boycotts to support the Southern sit-ins, a campaign to aid the victims of the Sharpeville massacre in South Africa, and anti-HUAC demonstrations which brought on the largest mass arrests theretofore in San Francisco and the literal baptism of hundreds of radicals by police fire hoses.

So, I'm talking about all of this to my brother, four years my senior, and he says he envies me, he wishes he were part of my generation. I thought, oh shit, what is he talking about, we are the same generation, we grew up together, we are brothers, not father and son.

But he was right. A new generation is born each year it seems. At the Washington antiwar protest the day before Richard Nixon's inauguration, Dave Dellinger introduced Jimmy Johnson, one of the Fort Hood Three, the first GIs to refuse to go to Vietnam, and who had just been released after two and a half years in

Leavenworth, to the demonstrators. Dellinger told the audience about the case of the Three: "A long long time ago, in 1966, when many of us were unaware of the Vietnam war. . . ."

During the 1968 struggle against the educational establishment and the teachers' union for community control of the New York school system, groups of high school kids throughout the city took to the streets to demonstrate support for their community leaders. Surviving brutality from the cops, distortion from the press, and provocation from the city government, the students emerged with a leadership far more politically sophisticated than we ever had when we were in college.

But if every year a new generation is born, every new generation sees its birth as the Year One of the whole movement. Bob Scheer of *Ramparts* and I, both in Havana for the tenth anniversary celebration of the Cuban Revolution, stayed up through one night recalling the early Berkeley movement. Tens of thousands have come and gone since then. Perhaps even hundreds of thousands. Very few have come the distance.

Scheer got to talking about Dr. King. And the thing about him, whatever his contradictions, whatever his mistakes, is that the man had staying power. He was key to the movement's beginning, and he remained key up to the day of his murder. Not only was he central to the movement, but he was often in its vanguard. Certainly he was in advance the day he went to Memphis to join the struggle for black liberation to the battle of sanitation workers.

Lots of folks in the movement today are talking about freedom, "by any means necessary." The quotation implies the gun. Now guns are fine in their place and may well be necessary. But the other means necessary may include, for one thing, going to work in a factory, and how many of us are prepared to go that route. If we are about the business of making fundamental change in these United States, we must understand it will be serious business. We are in for a long, difficult struggle.

The longevity of the movement depends in part upon historical perspective: To know from whence we come tells us something about where we should be heading. By the time this book reaches print, how many readers will have forgotten Rap Brown? How many will have even heard of Mario Savio? And for how great a majority is Caryl Chessman a case for only the archivists?

Following the fatal shootings of three black men outside the Republican national convention in August 1968, and the brutalities by Chicago police waged against demonstrators at the Democratic national convention three weeks later, a near agreement developed among media commentators. These actions and the Nixon and Humphrey nominations, together with the surprising popularity of the Wallace campaign, convinced the press that the nation was moving to the Right. The airways were jumping with talk of repression. Among the ranks of young radicals and hippies, and in black communities, talk became more specific. Concentration camps, they were saying. Would you believe it? Concentration camps.

The talk of a Great Repression has become a virtual roar compared to earlier warnings fifteen years ago by Communists and older radicals. How many of us would live through such a period? I mean *politically* live through such a period. This book is offered as the recollections of one who came into the movement in the late fifties, just barely avoiding being trampled by the rush of people leaving through the door I was entering. I suppose that makes me and my generation something of the Middle Left, chronologically speaking.

one

When I hear the word "culture," I reach for my revolver.
DOKTOR JOSEPH GOEBBELS

If I listened long enough to you
I'd find a way to believe that it's all true
Knowing that you lied straight-faced
While I cried
Still I look to find a reason to believe.
TIM HARDIN

For twenty years now, the President of the United States, whoever it might be at the time, has enjoyed the notion of himself as the Leader of the Free World. Consider now, if you will, what the cultural pursuits of these LFWs have been.

The Leader from Independence, Missouri, Harry S. Truman, liked the piano. He played the *Missouri Waltz* a lot. And his lovely Margaret sang. Sometimes the two would perform together. Then she went and married the managing editor of *The New York Times*, and moved away from home.

Former General Dwight Eisenhower, who learned to speak the English language passably for his farewell address after eight years as Leader, said he liked jazz. When the Prince of Thailand came to the White House on a visit of state, Ike learned that his guest was a jazz clarinetist. So the President generously arranged, for the Prince's listening pleasure, a concert by his (Ike's) favorite jazz musician—Guy Lombardo. Eisenhower also declared himself partial to Lawrence Welk. "I may not know art," said the Leader, "but I know what I like."

Jack Kennedy brought a breath of fresh air, and Leonard Bernstein, to the White House. He wanted the White House to be a courtly Palace of Culture and surrounded himself with the nation's most renowned jesters. Among the cultural personalities *not* invited to his soirées were Lenny Bruce, Nelson Algren, Charles Mingus and Paul Robeson. This Leader expressed a fondness for James Bond stories. His young Vassar-bred wife adored Truman Capote, Campbell Soup Can faddists, and whatever else was "current."

The Birdman of the Pedernales hailed from one of the best junior teachers' normals the whole wide state of Texas has to offer. Favoring Carol Channing in particular, LBJ had a special crush on the entire *Hello Dolly* show. After being disgusted by his official portrait as the "ugliest thing I ever saw," this Leader looked for spiritual guidance to Billy Graham.

Our present Leader takes his comfort from Norman Vincent Peale, demonstrating that he does indeed value Positive Thinking.

If one is to understand the development of a generation, it is helpful to know the cultural state of the nation during the years of its growth. The Leaders of the Free World provide some index of that state.

Consider our culture in the broader sense, not limited to the arts, but as a nation's way of life. When I was growing up in Los Angeles, I learned in school that: General MacArthur was the greatest American of the 20th century (I was made to stand in the cloak room for an hour for not demonstrating proper enthusiasm for the General on his triumphant tour of the city after being jerked out of Korea by President Truman for advocating bombing north of the Yalu); the Nazis weren't all bad, after all some of Hitler's own generals tried to kill him; black slaves in the South had it fair to middling under their owners who took care of them, their troubles began under Reconstruction; the Industrial Revolution began because Robert Fulton as a child watched his mother make tea, and applied the principles of the teapot to designing the steam engine and thus was born the Industrial Revolution, children. (I thought at the time, Where would we be if Mrs. Fulton liked espresso?). Although it may seem I exaggerate, it is the truth, I swear, as God Himself would verify, were he still alive.

Being reared near Hollywood, I was an intense movie devotee and every Saturday would go to the Holly theater (now torn down and replaced by the Citizens National Bank) or the Ramona, both on Sunset Boulevard (in approximately the same relation to Sunset in Hollywood as Riverdale's Broadway is to Times Square's) for ten cartoons, three serials and a movie about a good

Nazi. My favorite was about Werner von Braun, an officer in the SS and creator of the Reich's rocket program, now working for Our Team in Huntsville, Alabama. His biographical movie was called "I Aim for the Stars," which we subtitled, "And Hit England Instead."

A curious escapist culture came to envelop the Republic. When the stage, screen and radio were not glorifying the slaughter of Koreans or paying tribute to one ex-Communist stoolpigeon or another, the market was glutted with the grey-flannel phenomenon. A decade before Mike Harrington and the Kennedy family discovered poverty, this vapid fare extolled what was projected as the American Way of Life. We were a nation of junior executives who took the 5:22 home to Scarsdale, to be met by the little woman who waited with a decanter of martinis and the charcoals on the patio starting to heat. Not that we weren't "civic-minded"; the local Legion post and the Parent-Teachers Association occupied much of our extracurricular activities. We didn't talk to each other, but exchanged much gay banter. A country without serious problems, occasional "conflict" was lent the culture when flirtations with the neighbors' wives extended into extramarital "affairs."

An underground of pornographic paperbacks treating the same theme developed simultaneously: *Sin in Suburbia, Split-level Sex, My Neighbor's Wife*. The overground Culture of Death, while not as vulgar as the pulp paperbacks, was easily as obscene in its values. The white-collar fiction of Cheever, Salinger, Bellow and Updike held hegemony in the popular periodicals, graced every third suburban coffee table, and peppered the rows of those mobile public reading rooms known as subways.

Mana, for the commuter culture, was the Status Symbol. The lives of millions of Americans consisted of exchanging their talents for wampum to buy a vast collection of magical objects which bore no relation to actual physical needs, but which served to satisfy spiritual needs, pathetic though they were. Like the artifacts of the ancient Aztecs, the Status Symbol was representative of death. Especially, as one observer noted, the dead mistress under the Arden dryer. The hero of the day was Willie Loman, who earnestly held that, "It's not what you do. . . . It's who you know and the smile on your face. It's contacts. . . . The man who makes an appearance in the business world, the man who creates personal interest, is the man who gets ahead. Be liked and you will never want."

My hometown being Los Angeles, I was growing up absurd in the kitsch capital of this America. Someone once described Hollywood as a black 22-foot Caddie moving along Sunset Boulevard, with a long elegant feminine arm sticking out. The arm, encased in an elbow-length glove, supports a diamond bracelet, and holds a half-eaten bagel. If the national psyche was on the lam, there could be no better sanctuary than the wide open spaces of Southern California. If the 1848 search for California gold was a rush, the crush a century later reached stampede proportions. Came they did: the lame, the halt, the blind, the dazed, the crazed. Miss California was Miss America. The queen of flesh was traditionally from Indiana, a Wasp. Personalityless, sexless, deodorized young womanhood, appealing to all, offending none, reigning over the hearts of us all, she had moved from Terre Haute to Los Angeles. She still loved Mom and Dad and fudge brownies, but now the latter were the kind prescribed by Alice B. Toklas, and the former were put out, because they discovered that daughter put out, at the drive-in theater.

Though she never happened out my way, Charlotte Ford, daughter of Henry the Second, and one year my junior, always appealed to me as an Angeleno of the sort the media made out in those days to be just folks. Since junior high school, I followed in the Los Angeles *Times* with great fascination the latest exploits of my generational soul sister. I thrilled with her as I read of her debut in Detroit, "which cost about $250,000 and took more than a year to plan, and was attended by 1,200 guests. The cost of flowers alone was put at $60,000. Two million magnolia leaves were flown from Mississippi for the party and were used to cover the walls of the corridors leading to the reception room in the Country Club of Detroit, which had been redecorated to resemble an eighteenth-century French chateau."

And how elated we all were to read of her joining the Movement in 1963. That being the Year of the Problem, with the March on Washington and Jimmy Baldwin making the cover of *Time*, Miss Ford could not keep silent. No matter what your station in life, she told *The New York Times'* society page, one could not remain aloof from the burning question of the day. Yet, she felt, she was in a position to make a unique contribution towards the solution of the problem, and so she would like to announce her plans to open up a $40,000 mobile good-grooming clinic in Harlem.

The Times later found fit to print the news that she "wears her hair long, has been listed several times as one of the world's twelve best-dressed women. She does not drink and she smokes only one or two cigarettes a day. She has been active in social and philanthropic causes, most notably the Police Athletic League, and has worked as an interior decorator." The description came with the report of Charlotte's eloping with Greek shipping magnate Stavros Niarchos, 32 years her senior. Wrote *The Times*, "The announcement of the surprise wedding was made here in the name of Miss Ford's father and her mother, Mrs. Anne McDonnell Ford, first wife of Mr. Ford. The bride's father is eight years younger than his 56-year-old son-in-law. . . . Miss Ford's parents first learned of her marriage on Wednesday night. Neither attended the ceremony. Miss Ford, an attractive blonde, and the darkly handsome shipping executive, were married in Juarez by Civil Register Judge Baltazar Aguirre. The bride, a Roman Catholic, was unable to marry Mr. Niarchos in a religious ceremony because of his two divorces. Her father, the head of the Ford Motor Company, was excommunicated last February when he married Mrs. Maria Christina Vettore Austin after he divorced Miss Ford's mother. . . . Mr. Niarchos was divorced Wednesday morning, presumably in Mexico, from his second wife."

Within a short time Charlotte had separated from Niarchos and given birth to their child, several weeks too premature for "respectability." The Ford Foundation, we recall, helps sponsor Daniel Moynihan's Urban Affairs Center discover that the urban black family is often a wreck. In any case, Charlotte Ford has meant a great deal to my political development. She will always be Miss America to me.

When I was in high school, the most popular cultural experience in the United States, shared by scores of millions across the land, was watching a jockey answer questions about painting, or some child psychiatrist, or an "arctic explorer," or a Hassidic Jew from Brooklyn, or a Columbia University instructor, each trying to parlay their avocations into $64,000. It was about this time that the denomination "egghead" was popularized to indicate one of intellectual bent. The Adlai Stevenson candidacy and, a few years later, Soviet Sputnik I made human use of the thought process ripe for acceptance in that dreary decade. Academics were once again making out their applications for admittance into the American family.

With the decline of Ringling Brothers, Clyde Beatty, Frank Buck, and Barnum and Bailey, the Big Top was about to be pulled down. Then a network idea man dreamed up the *$64,000 Question.* As Dalton Trumbo asked at the time, "Who cares to estimate how many millions of savage little juveniles, denied their nightly beakers of blood, twisted sullenly while the old man roared his answers at the sweating slob on the TV screen, and mother filled the station breaks with gentle sermons on the cash value of education?" Until some fink, underpaid for his part in the fix, went and blew the proverbial whistle on the quiz show racket. One earlier contestant explained that he was not yet "convinced" that taking a dive was "fraudulant." One of the producers allowed as how he was "trying to put together an exciting and interesting show and I never did feel there was anything terribly wrong with it." Another participant declared, "I feel perfectly blithe about it . . . They were having a happy time, I was, everybody was."

The scandal passed quickly enough. A peculiar national psychology had developed with the Cold war. We acquiesced. Noted Trumbo, "We expect the news to be slanted; we expect the statesman to lie; we expect the politician to make deals; we expect the advertisement to be false; we expect the repairman to cheat us; we expect the fight to be fixed; we expect men to place self-interest above any conceivable social end." The nation may have deplored the quiz show incident when children were present, but more often than not, it displayed a warped admiration for the audacity of the networks.

Midcentury United States, the setting in which I came of age, had grown accustomed to the acne of corruption which speckled its face. The Mayor of New York, William O'Dwyer, had to make a fast getaway to Mexico when some of the city's more obvious operations came to public light. That he was just named Ambassador to Mexico made that country the obvious choice for his new haven. And how many of us remember Sherman Adams, kindly old Ike's principal advisor? How many days did he and Bernard Goldfine, his partner in crime, spend in the jug?

And while professional sport has scarcely kept secret that it is about as riddled with ideals as the narcotics traffic, it has maintained a pose of having a corner on honesty east of Iowa. But in the fifties, boxing took a nosedive. The fix had just been in a bit too long. Like any successful business enterprise, it hopelessly underpaid its help. The professional athlete is nothing so much as an indentured servant who's allowed out at night. He is barred from thinking out loud, certainly not in the presence of an alert reporter. In other, lesser fields of endeavor, like education or science or art, this sort of pressure is called censorship, and the natives get restless and talk about freedom and that sort of crap. Not in sports. Fighters were paid to win; some were paid to lose. None were paid to talk, because that task is performed by money. (A decade later, Muhammed Ali came along to raise the hopes and interests of another generation, but not understanding the rules, he was evicted from the game.)

Okay, let's see. What else had an impact on my adolescent mind? There was former U.S. Senator Arthur V. Watkins of Utah, who as chief of the Indian Claims Commission, told a group of Pit River Indians in Northern California who were pressing a land claim: "I'm tired of hearing you slam this country. I am proud of America and you should be too. This is the first time a subject people have ever been permitted to sue the Nation that conquered them. I think this is a fine mark of democracy."

There was the Reverend Claude Carter of Stockton, who after years of officiating at the Stockton, California, Healing Temple, was busted on rape charges, based on relations with three parishioners, ages eight, eleven and sixteen. Preaching that wives should abstain from their husbands and yield only to him, he described this procedure as "building to God." A man of obvious conviction in days of a breakdown of public morality and trust, the Reverend Carter practiced what he preached. From the Stockton jail, he proclaimed, "The Bible said those who help others will be falsely accused." Said one of the men in his flock, "Sure I knew there was something going on between the Reverend and my wife but I liked what the man had to say."

A nation given to the spectacular, we did not give much notice to 34-year-old El Paso car salesman William Pettit, who was charged with statutory rape of a fifteen-year-old girl he allegedly seduced five times atop a 65-foot-high flagpole. Pettit had spent 64 days on top of the flagpole as an advertising stunt. The young girl, name withheld, apparently ran herself up the flagpole to see if anyone would salute her. Five times.

Raised in Los Angeles, a town noted for advanced police methods, I was also impressed with the vigor of law enforcement in Portland, Oregon. When Mary Eggers, 29, despondent about her health, climbed onto the ledge of her fourth-floor hotel room and threatened to jump, alert Portland patrolmen sneaked up behind and pulled her back. Then they took her into custody, charging despondent Miss Eggers with disorderly conduct.

"America," wrote Allen Ginsburg, when I was a high school junior, "I've given you all and now I'm nothing. . . . America when will you be Angelic?/When will you take off your clothes? . . . America why are your libraries full of tears? . . . I'm sick of your insane demands./When can I go into the supermarket and buy what I need with my good looks? . . . America I used to be a communist when I was a kid I'm not sorry. . . . I'm addressing you./Are you going to let your emotional life be run by Time Magazine?" But the Republic, whose mentality had reached the point where today it can allow itself to burn babies alive in southeast Asia, and become unhinged at the sight of young men with long hair, has in fact had its emotional life run by Henry Luce.

So the Poet could say, in the most widely accepted and profoundly accurate description of the 1950's, "I saw the best minds of my generation destroyed by madness, starving hysterical naked." As if to say that the minds of his generation have also been destroyed by madness, Dr. William C. Menninger, perhaps the nation's best-known psychiatrist, announced that emotional or mental illness affects "one out of one of us." The layman's recognition of mental illness encompasses only gross generalizations like "nervous breakdown," "combat fatigue" and "shell shock," he said. "None of these laymen's terms include his tension headaches, his marital discords, his private worries about the business, his dependency on alcohol or nicotine." The doctor said that the severe mental illnesses which require hospitalization affect one out of twelve Americans during their lifetime. In addition, some 800,000 of those with neuroses—incapacitating illnesses not requiring hospitalization—consult psychiatric clinics and private psychiatrists. There are some 4.5 million alcoholics from sea to shining sea, and according to the good doctor, "Fifty percent of medical practice has to do with some 17.5 million persons with conversion symptoms; headaches, gastro-intestinal disorders, and 'Oh, my aching back.' These persons have difficulties that should receive some psychiatric treatment."

The really hopeless victims of mental illness are to be found among those who appear to be most normal. As Erich Fromm wrote: "Many of them are normal because they are so well adjusted to our mode of existence, because their human voice has been silenced so early in their lives, that they do not even struggle or suffer or develop symptoms as the neurotic does."

"Think," wrote an executive in the 1950's, "of what it can mean to your firm in profits if you can condition a million or ten million children, who will grow up into adults trained to buy your product, as soldiers and trained in advance when they hear the trigger words, Forward March!" * And so we were trained in advance. No nursery rhymes for us. Instead: You'll wonder where the yellow went, when you brush your teeth with Pepsodent.

During my teenage years, Vance Packard's *The Hidden Persuaders* dominated the bestseller lists, with its descriptions of subliminal brain-washing techniques being experimented with by advertisers. The latest cheerful ecstasies about new discoveries in laxatives could now be impressed on the mind as it was engrossed in a soap-opera lover's embrace. Amusement and resignation

* As quoted by Aldous Huxley in *Brave New World Revisited*.

greeted the hidden persuaders. Certainly not outrage. Again we acquiesced.

A half-dozen years ago, in 1963 the President of the United States was murdered. For three days running, 50 million television sets were tuned into Dallas, Texas. Among the sights they were treated to were: the live murder of the alleged assassin inside the Dallas jail, by a small-time pimp, in the presence of a score of Dallas' finest;* the FBI, the CIA, the Secret Service and the Dallas Police contradicting each other and themselves, changing their stories a dozen times, each time with greater conviction and certainty; the new First Lady directing the interior decoration of her new home, and the removal of the remnants of the White House's previous residents; and a whole nation of people in mourning for a man who had brought them closer to thermonuclear incineration than anyone else before or since.

Since that day, every poll taken shows that maybe one in three people in this country believes the official story of the incident, as pronounced by the then Chief Justice of the U.S. Supreme Court, the Director of the FBI, and the President of the United States and Leader of the Free World. In Europe, claim U.S. apologists, "nobody believes us." *Life* magazine, the Governor of Texas who was wounded in the same car as the murdered president, the senior Senator from Connecticut, and a dozen best-selling books, have all called for a new investigation of the assassination.

And just about nobody believes there will ever be one.

* Television executives recently announced that if the Vietnam war lasts through 1970, we can expect live coverage of the battles. One wonders, should the war receive a low Trendex rating, will Washington cancel it?

two

"English *history!*" *roared the silver-maned
senior senator from his state indignantly. "What's the
matter with American history? American history
is as good as any history in the world!"*

—Catch-22

*If I have to push the button that
will kill 100,000 people—well,
you need values in a situation like that.*
      —A MIDSHIPMAN, *quoted in* Harper's Magazine

What I have pictured are just a few threads of a whole fabric of a life-system gone mad. Now, I've never been much for literary theory. Discussions of naturalism vs. realism vs. modernism have never seemed very interesting or particularly important to me. But if one was to paint the reality in the United States of my years, one would have to paint the reality of a system gone mad, it seems to me. *Catch-22* and *One Flew Over the Cuckoo's Nest* may well be the most realistic novels of my generation. And if Charlie Chaplin was the comic genius of the pre-World War II generation, capturing the essence of his time with humor, compassion and a sense of the tragic, then Lenny Bruce is our postwar comic genius for the same reasons. The madness exiled Charlie; it killed Lenny; it kills a lot of us.

The madness became official U.S. Government policy at the end of the war, and remains so today. Some years ago, a group of gentlemen—Walter Lippmann, Adlai Stevenson, Henry Luce and others—set out to define the National Purpose. But they and their contemporaries had already defined it for me and my contemporaries. It was to Destroy the Red Menace. In school, in church, on radio, even in skywriting (at least in Los Angeles, a town with a flair for this sort of thing), we got the message. The passwords to acceptance were "I am not now nor have I ever been." The only viable alternative was, "I was and here is a list of who else was."

Not since a century before, when the Ku Klux Klan was built by placing the stamp of tawdry nobility on all who were not black, had virtue been determined not on the basis of what one was, but on what one was not. In 1966, when nineteen Minutemen were busted in Queens on their way to blow up three summer camps and Communist historian Herbert Aptheker's office in Brooklyn, their families exclaimed, "They're good boys, not Communists." Among others who were not nor ever had been Communists were the members of the board of directors of Standard Oil of New

Jersey, the several hundred-thousand dope pushers infecting the nation, the Mafia, the National Association of Manufacturers, the Veterans of Foreign Wars leadership, and the herds of pimps working their wares in every urban center.

Loyalty oaths and disclaimers cared not if the signatory was a sadist, fascist, bunko artist, racist, stoolpigeon, FBI director, medical quack, munitions profiteer, media gossip-monger, or any of a gross of other free world professions. Only if you belonged to the Communist Party. One could mark cards, load dice, lecher high and low, steal pencils from blind peddlers or quarters off the eyes of the dead, one could kick one's mother. But one entered the company of the Blessed if one was not now nor ever had been.

The Nation could take satisfaction during the quiz-show scandal in the knowledge that all who participated in the fraud were certified as loyal Americans. The networks had used their elaborate system of clearing their backgrounds through HUAC, the Attorney General, FBI, Senate Internal Security Subcommittee, *Red Channels,* sponsor's snoops, agency private dicks, and scores of other weird people who dig looking into cracks for a living. Wrote Dalton Trumbo: "The people who dived, and the people who won, and all who arranged the cheat and sponsored it, and distributed it, had never been controversial; they had never publicly dissented from anything; they had never joined a *verboten* organization; they had never given money to unpopular causes. To the last child they were authenticated patriots, well-oathed and clean as the whistle that finally blew them up. Though tens of millions of dollars were earned by sponsors, broadcasters, and producers of the fraudulent shows, though the trust of a nation's children was ravished by them, at least the Republic could take comfort that it hadn't been gulled by a gang of subversives."

In an era when hundreds of thousands were blacklisted (and remain so) from the entertainment industry, teaching and research, government service and union leadership; were deported, beaten, jailed and threatened with jail; when two were murdered in the electric chair at Ossining; in those years of the Red Menace when the present Leader rode to fame in a pumpkin shell; when Secretary of Defense James V. Forrestal chose to be Dead rather than Red and jumped from a Miami hotel to execute his choice; when the junior Senator who lent his name to the era had the names of 219 Communist agents in the State Department; when the drugstore liberal who later rose to the Vice-Presidency proposed to make the Communist Party illegal and to set up concentration camps should the "need" for them arise; at this point in our national pastoral, the market—TV, movies, books—was glutted with the stoolpigeon culture. Matt Cvetic was a Communist for the FBI and Herbert Philbrick led three lives.

NBC invited Whittaker Chambers to read, over nationwide hookup, his "Letter to His Children," and the *Saturday Evening Post* serialized his memoirs, billing it "one of the great books of our time." Not since the Roman Emperor Tiberius erected statues to informers, had a nation paid down its tribute to those who lie and snoop for pieces of silver. Now the State of Massachusetts held an annual Philbrick Day. Chambers received 75 grand from the *Post* for his tale. Harvey Matusow, Elizabeth Bentley, Louis Budenz* and assorted other professional perjurers became the picadors drawing first blood for their congressional superiors as the crowd, tasting the heady maddening wine of human slaughter, screamed for the kill. The nation watched as the sun began to set on the American empire.

In later years, the country began somewhere along the line to inch itself toward sanity. That is when a new danger faced Our Great Nation; the credibility gap began. If one could pinpoint the moment, it may well have been when Francis Gary Powers and his "weather" plane "strayed" 2,000 miles into the Soviet Union only

---

* Among the more notable figures in the corps of government informers.

to get promptly knocked out of the sky by alert antiaircraft. The cat was out of the bag, and this particular feline's name was CIA. All of its litter followed in line quickly enough: Playa Girón, Tonkin Gulf, National Student Association, Meany-Lovestone, Grayson Kirk. By the time of the Pueblo capture off the shore of Korea, Murray Kempton could write, "I believe the North Koreans, personally. They haven't been lying to me lately." The credibility gap had widened to abyss proportions.

For myself, I had very little time to develop illusions about the state of the nation, so I never really did become disillusioned. I think my own personal credibility gap with the establishment developed irretrievably one night when I was about eleven or twelve. My best friend at the time, the son of an L.A. cop, invited me over to watch television inasmuch as, being out of step with American culture's iron heel, my family hadn't yet bought a TV. I was culturally deprived. The evening fare at that time was Philbrick's *I Led Three Lives*. The point of this particular episode was that the Reds look just like you and me, and live in regular neighborhoods, so therefore keep a careful eye on your neighbors. It showed how, at Party "cell" meetings, in order to avoid drawing the attention of neighbors to the fact that a gathering was taking place down the block, members had to enter and leave the meeting singularly at ten-minute intervals. The televised drama showed a meeting of about two dozen comrades. My excellent training through the Los Angeles school system enabled me to figure that it took some eight hours just to gather and disperse from the meeting. Either the Reds were even weirder than Philbrick was letting on, or the star witness was lying. Figuring that no organization, no matter how subversive, could dominate the country as we were led to believe the Communist Party was doing, with such obvious time-consuming inefficiency, my budding teenage mind told me that the fink was being less than honest. And if he was a fink for the government, then not all was on the up and up in Washington. At the age of twelve, I was already estranged from the free world leadership.

Growing up in a section of Los Angeles called East Hollywood (as Hoboken might be called West Manhattan), movie stars were naturally in my eyes. Kids in the neighborhood would try to go to professional child-actor training schools. The high school through which I suffered contained the offspring of a number of the famed and infamed. When the un-Americans came to Hollywood I became terribly excited. My father had been working as a set designer for a number of the major studios. We had recently moved from Washington D.C., where he had practiced his chosen profession, architecture. In the studios, he became active in the organization of the studio union, which pulled off the first major strike to actively challenge the recently passed Taft-Hartley Law. As a result, he was arrested along with several hundred others and blacklisted from the rolls of studio employables.

When HUAC came to Hollywood, the city fathers responded in Cecil B. De Mille fashion. Among the committee members was a new local boy from the bushes, Richard M. Nixon, who had only recently made the big leagues. Of course he has since risen to new depths but at the time he was only a rhinestone in the rough. Accompanying Congressman Nixon was Representative John E. Rankin of Mississippi, an animated Feiffer cartoon if there's ever been one. In response to a protest against the committee by a group of Hollywood personalities, Rankin would say: "They sent this petition to Congress, and I want to read you some of these names. One of the names is June Havoc. We found out . . . that her real name is June Hovick. Another one was Danny Kaye, and we found out his real name was David Daniel Kamirsky. . . . There is one who calls himself Edward Robinson. His real name is Emanuel Godenberg. There is another one here who calls himself Melvyn Douglas, whose real name is Melvyn Hesselberg. There are others too numerous to mention. They are attacking the Committee for doing its duty to protect this country and save the American people from the horrible fate the Communists have meted out to the unfortunate *Christian* people of Europe." (Emphasis added.)

Others launching political careers at the Hollywood pad included then leading men George Murphy and Ronald Reagan, who served as friendly witnesses for the Committee. Murphy, a particular favorite of mine, could declare in his successful campaign for U.S. Senate, a decade and a-half after naming the desirous names, "The civil rights record in California is excellent. I don't know where in the state there have been many problems."

Subpoenaed before the Committee were nineteen unfriendly witnesses, only ten of whom testified, or rather refused to. Had the others been called and the Hollywood Ten been instead the Hollywood Nineteen, they would have included the obviously un-American Berthold Brecht and Charles Chaplin. Sensing the degree of charity residing in the Committee, both took off for their native lands, never to return to free American soil. One observer noted, regarding Brecht, "He seemed to have the uncomfortable feeling, based, perhaps, on earlier hassles over un-German activities, that all those doctors of humane letters who earned their bread by writing about his plays and describing his genius, would forget, somehow, to set the alarm clock on the day he went to jail."

Because it was not the Nixons and Reagans, the Rankins and Joe McCarthys who averred that the best way to fight the Committee was to ostracize those who did. It was a job for sheep in sheep's clothing, not wolves, as Dalton Trumbo pointed out. Wrote Trumbo, the most prominent of the Ten:

It was Arthur M. Schlesinger, Jr.'s 'non-Communist Left' bursting out of the river and crossing the trees in its first wild stampede to-

ward the Center, startling to their feet great herds of creeping Social-
ists, while Max Eastman and Sidney Hook, riding the flanks and
bearing down hard, fired buckshot and bacon rind at the face of the
wondering moon.

They were going so fast they overshot their mark, but toward
dawn they found themselves in some pretty fair pastureland slightly
to the right of center. The grass was ankle-high, there was a stream
to drink from and defecate into, the horses were winded and they
were all bone-tired, so they decided to settle in permanently. Bugles
blared, enlisted men stood at attention, and censors swung great pots
of diabolofuge, and the chief idealogue christened the place Vital
Center. After the songs were finished they proclaimed a new alphabet
and sent guerrilla bands fanning out through the countryside in all
directions. They had been secretly trained to throw aspersions instead
of cast them, their aim was deadly, and whenever they scored a hit
they swarmed down on the poor devil and forced him to draw his
own conclusions in the mire, while everybody stood around and
jeered. By the time they were through you couldn't cross the Charles
River without three salutes and a police permit.

Some years after the Hollywood Ten were out of jail, Frank
Sinatra announced that he was hiring Albert Maltz to write the
screenplay of *The Execution of Private Slovik*. Shortly afterward,
Sinatra announced in *Variety* that he was rescinding his decision
because, "the American public has indicated it feels the morality
of hiring Albert Maltz is a more crucial matter, and I will accept
this majority." Sinatra's "majority" on the moral factor consisted
entirely of the American Legion and his friend Jack Kennedy,
then a candidate for President. The *Variety* announcement, a
monument to Frankie's lack of clout, placed him alongside the
Schlesingers in reinforcing the repression of McCarthyism.

As did the spectacle of Lucille Ball, shown bawling on wire-
service photos and network news program across the nation, as it
was revealed she had signed a petition to place the Communist

Party on the ballot in 1932. She did it all for grandpa, she explained. The old man's politics matched his granddaughter's famous head of hair, but she didn't know what she was doing at that young age. No such qualification could be made as, now in full maturity, she disassociated herself from the grandfather for whom she had signed that dangerous petition 25 years before. I loved this Lucy a good deal less than another, first name Autherine, the first black student "integrated" into the University of Alabama, just weeks after Lucille Ball wept for herself and her Trendex rating.

In one of history's more wonderful bits of irony, the Soviet Union did indeed dictate moral standards in the United States at the height of a national hysteria against Communism. So that when Autherine Lucy was expelled from college, that was declared "a victory for Communism." The struggle against segregation was launched not to eradicate this throwback to the days of antebellum chattel, but so as not to "play directly into the hands of the Reds." Since 1919, the year of its founding, the U.S. Communist Party fought for a Supreme Court ruling against segregation, but when *Brown vs. the Board of Education* was decided, editorials proclaimed that "a mortal blow" had been struck against Communism, which has survived more than its share of mortal blows.

Now, how crazy can you get is a disputable question, but the United States was mobilized to make a national effort to rewrite the record book. Intellectual pursuits made a U-turn in fortune when Sputnik I was launched. We had to have better schools so as not to lose a crucial battle to Communism. In the natural order of things now, boy would kiss girl, whispering fervently, "I do this not out of love for you but by doing so I am registering my opposition to nefarious Communism." In 1967, Arthur Schlesinger, Jr., announced that the time had come to blow the whistle on those "cold war revisionists"—historians who had placed the major burden for the cold war on the United States. Most of these, starting with Sir P.M.S. Blackett, indicate that the U.S. dropped the atom bombs on Hiroshima and Nagasaki not to hasten the war's end but to warn the Soviet Union, approaching Japan from the West, not to go too far. The hundreds of thousands incinerated and permanently maimed in history's only atomic attacks could suffer more easily in the knowledge that the Soviet Union never really got into the Asian theatre of operations. As could, in the most logical extension of this policy, the women and children of Ben Tre, South Vietnam, who were slaughtered as their homes were wiped off the map because, as the U.S. officer in charge explained, "We had to destroy the town in order to save it."

For my childhood, the names of Auschwitz, Nuremburg, Hiroshima, Seoul, and Guatemala were pedagogical. They said to a young mind that there was a new ethic sweeping the "civilized" world, one which allowed for genocide in the name of security from the forces of evil. I could laugh when I'd read about the doctor going around to all the branch libraries in L.A., a list of key anti-Communist books—by Hoover, Chambers, Cvetic—in hand. He'd find out which of the books were checked out and overdue for return, then publish a list of the overdue offenders as Communists trying to keep the works out of circulation. But the laughter thinned out when Eddie Rickenbacker, board chairman of Eastern Airlines and World War I air ace, could talk about the "diabolical Mongolian philosophy called Communism." Or when the National Association of Real Estate Boards began to circulate bumper stickers bearing the legend "Join the American Revolution . . . Freedom Forever Under God." At the realtors' national convention in Miami Beach, debate ensued over the slogan. Some wondered if it was not a mistake to use the word "Revolution" in the service of a patriotic group. The chairman replied that others had also objected, but he believed that the meaning was safely conveyed by the additional words "Under God."

This new Christianity was of a vintage familiar in earlier

annals, when others were thrown to the lions and the audience retired to a feast and orgy. Whittaker Chambers, in his *Saturday Evening Post* memoirs, wrote that his severance with Communism began when, staring at his baby daughter's ears he was struck with the thought, "No, those ears were not created by any chance coming together of atoms in nature (the Communist view). They could have been created only by immense design." Communism, he wrote, "is what happens when in the name of Mind, men free themselves from God."

J. Edgar Hoover, the Ghost of Cotton Mather Past, laid down this indictment in *Christianity Today*:

In a dingy London apartment, a garrulous, haughty and intolerant atheist, Karl Marx, callous to the physical sufferings and poverty of his family, was busy mixing the ideological acids of this evil philosophy. Originally of interest only to skid row debaters and wandering minstrels of revolution, Marx's pernicious doctrines were given organization power by a beady-eyed Russian, V. I. Lenin. . . .

Communist morality, of course, is rooted in total rejection of a belief in God and in the values of the Christian moral code. . . . This rejection of God gives Communism a demonic aspect— transforming it into a fanatical, Satanic, brutal phenomenon. . . .

Communism represents a new age of barbarism, which is repealing the centuries of progress of Western man toward tolerance, understanding, and human brotherhood. Communist Man . . . is truly an alarming monster, human in physical form, but in practice a cynically godless and immoral machine. . . .

Like an epidemic of polio, the solution lies not in minimizing the danger or overlooking the problem—but rapidly, positively, and courageously finding an anti-polio serum. We in America have this anti-Communism serum, the answer to the Communist challenge. It lies in *the strength of our Judaic-Christian tradition, the power of the Holy Spirit working in men.* . . . (Italics, JEH.)

In the final analysis, the Communist world view must be met and defeated by the Christian world view.

So our national way of life became a religion that pitted our Ultimate Godliness against Godless Satan. There was no room for dialogue. There was to be no rest, no peace, until the antipolio serum was administered. The proof of the passion became Vietnam. (Read Dr. Tom Dooley on Laos and Vietnam.) If it had become necessary to kill children, then we surely would kill them, and in substantial quantities. But it was not children we incinerated in Vietnam; it was Communist children.

three

"Watch out, the ears have walls."
— GRAFFITTI

Said Officer MacDougal in dismay:
"The force can't do a decent job
'Cause the kids got no respect
For the law today (and blah blah blah)."
"Save the life of my child!"
Cried the desperate mother.
"What's becoming of the children?"
People asking each other.
— PAUL SIMON and ART GARFUNKEL

As a concession to the autobiographical aspects of this book, I should say that most of my early childhood memories, sketchy at best, are of a political nature. The few things I remember, all connected to The War, are mixed with irrelevant personal events which help retain the former in my mind. I recall, for example, seeing *30 Seconds Over Tokyo* with Van Johnson, when I was three, but it sticks with me because I fell out of the family car on the way to the theatre, the goose egg developing on my forehead complementing the anti-Fascist drama on the screen. And I remember seeing General Chenault's Flying Tigers circling high over my schoolyard, because that was the day I was skipped out of kindergarten and into the first grade. Air raid warnings—the dimming of lights, the black curtains being pulled over windows—come back to me because my little brother was born on a day there was an alert, and because my father was an air raid warden. Seeing all those grown-ups crying in the streets of Washington is what I remember of the day FDR died. Since that April day when I was four, my folks haven't had a President they could call their own.

I was told by my mother that we were moving to Los Angeles to cure my big brother's asthma, but I now suspect an equal consideration was that the cold war was settling down in Washington, having accepted a permanent position as personnel director for government jobs, and that we got out while the getting was good. Shortly after arriving in Greater Disneyland, I was enrolled in a grammar school which provided copy for *Life* twice in the short time my presence graced the campus. The principal first came to the attention of the Luce empire as the innovator of the "red alert," a phenomenon that swept the nation's school systems at a gallop. This was a new kind of preparation, to accompany the familiar fire drill, for the imminent invasion of the Soviet Red Army, and consisted of crouching on hands and knees under your desk for thirty seconds. It hardly seemed adequate for the impending doom, it occurred to me. *Life* photographers also gave play to the schoolyard which, in after-hours, served as the home-base for what the magazine called the second (or maybe third) most dangerous juvenile gang in the country. The gang members' kid brothers and sisters, all Mexican or Italian, my playmates, were referred to by Tex, the playground director, as "beans" and "dagos"; I was the only "wooge."

My only other grammar school memories were my father's bust in the studio strike; my aforementioned passive resistance to the national passion play around General McArthur; my tonsil-adenoid operation and its mention on the *Uncle Whoa Bill* radio program; my one-man epidemic of bee stings, nine in one week; and my appearances on the Art Linkletter show. One of the fringe benefits of growing up in L.A. was the possibility of momentary fame as fatherly Art led you into making *faux pas* for the listening pleasure of the nation's housewives. A CBS limousine would come by the school early in the day to pick up a half-dozen of us, and take us to the Brown Derby for lunch. Then, at the studio, we would be briefed as to what we should say by one of the producer's assistants. These prepared ad-libs served to provoke the mirth of a gaggle of geriatrics from the Atlantic to the Pacific.

Junior high school brings to mind my folks hiding controversial books in the linen closet as Richard Nixon got the vice-presidential nomination. Where there's smoke, there's salmon, they figured. My junior high school time capsule also includes praise from liberal teachers for my belonging to the same gang as Chicano and Chinese classmates. When I once asked what they were praising, I was told: "Your tolerance." "Tolerance" was very much the liberal thing in those pre-Montgomery days. On graduation day, I was scheduled to give a speech, being one of the student government officers. A last-minute switch relegated me to the role of ersatz master-of-ceremonies. My prepared speech was unacceptable, I was told, because most of the audience would not understand my references to John Peter Zenger, Thomas Paine, and Frederick Douglass. I had also noted that that day marked the first anniversary of the execution of Julius and Ethel Rosenberg.

I could never understand my high school teachers telling me that these were the best years of my life. Easily the most miserable three years I have ever spent, I was prepared to make them my last if the teachers' predictions had been true. A year and a-half ahead of myself in school, through being skipped at an early age, all my friends were two and three years older. In the best of circumstances, adolescence is awkward; in my situation, I had a permanent feeling much as if I was exposing myself at a coronation. My friends from junior high had gone to a different high school than mine. Making the best of a dreadful situation, I ran for student government and played basketball for the school team my first year, setting records at neither activity. My older brother had been student body president the year before I entered and had more than made a mark for himself. At the student government meeting following my election, the principal came in to announce to the gathered young solons that "We've had one red Myerson here, and that was one too many." This minor embarrassment was followed by disaster: my first true love went down to bitter defeat. To a Hammett fan like me, it looked like the Big Casino.

I became a *borachon*. The next couple of years were the longest lost weekend in John Marshall High School history. What I couldn't finish drinking at night was poured down the morning after. My two best friends, both Mexican, relied on my Yankee ingenuity to come up with creations like oranges, filled with vodka by hypodermic syringe, which we would devour throughout the school day. When we went to school. A few years older than me, they would provide me with excitement and I would do their schoolwork for them. Harrassing the teachers and administration to the point of hysteria, we were premature Provos. Constant subpoenas to the principal's office, suspensions, even arrests, reached their zenith on graduation day, when I was expelled six hours before the ceremonies for bringing a case of beer to a favorite teacher.

The next day, running downhill at age sixteen, I fled to Mexico, on the pretext of going to the university. My closest friend, son of the Mexican Consul to Los Angeles, came with me and we lived with his family. What began as an endless drinking bout came to a sudden halt. I'm not sure why, but a number of things happened about the same time. One day I was traveling through the countryside on a third-class bus. The only other rider was a woman, perhaps twenty years of age, who looked as if her best years were well behind her. It's not at all uncommon to find Mexican women breast-feeding in public, so I took no note of the obvious suckling under her *rebozo*. After about twenty minutes, however, the noise grew to agonized screeches. Another quarter-hour of the unbearable bleats passed, and the young woman got off the bus. Re-adjusting her shawl, she allowed the creature out for air. A pig! She was breast-feeding a pig because she couldn't afford food to otherwise keep it alive.

Fidel Castro and 81 comrades had recently left Mexico to begin what would become perhaps the major political influence on the lives of my contemporaries. Mexican students were already throbbing with the prospects of the July 26th Movement, and talk of a new Mexican Revolution was beginning. A strike of architecture students was organized, the first in years. Petroleum workers and teachers also struck. The contrast of this intense activity with the States of McCarthy and Eisenhower which I had just left was striking. Mexico City resembled nothing so much as my favorite cinematic capital, *Casablanca,* teeming with exiled revolutionaries—from Spain, Venezuela, Guatemala—and with FBI and CIA agents, adventurers and stoolpigeons. Unfounded rumors of armed uprisings abounded, and student friends of mine prepared for any eventuality by building caches of arms. At one point, a friend and I started by motorcycle to Guatemala, only to be halted by the news that dictator Castillo Armas had been assassinated and the border closed to entry or exit. On returning to the city, an earthquake hit the interior, causing some 500 deaths in the Federal District alone. A movie house around the corner from where I stayed collapsed, killing a dozen persons. Three blocks away, a six-story apartment house crumbled. Telephone and telegraph communications were cut. The government sent out a call for all available men. I showed up and was ordered to direct traffic in a nearby district. Poor families living in one-room dirt-floor hovels, protected only by "doors" made of bedsheets, were now forced into the streets. The facts of Mexican life had sobered me up.

Back in Los Angeles, I enrolled at City College for a semester. Working its way up from *City Lights* and *Evergreen Review* into the pages of *Time* and *Esquire,* the Beat Generation became the publishing world's pin-up of the year 1957–8. San Fernando suburbanites flocked in cashmere turtlenecks to Hollywood clubs to hear "poetry and jazz." The entrepreneur in me rose to the fore and I founded the "Avant Guarde Poets" at school, made up only of myself. Scratching out a dozen verses in about an hour, I sent them in to the college newspaper just to see what the market would bear. The most obvious kind of put-on (my older brother's favorite line was "Juan Peron is the Abominable Snowman of Levittown"), a couple of the "poems" were printed. Jazz pianists Les McCann and Hamp Hawes, both fellow students, were approached, and we were going to give a concert to make some bread, but even I couldn't quite bring myself to fling that *chozzerai* at 1,200 paying customers. But I did get a couple of professors to testify to the "brilliance and great promise" of the poems and poet, respectively. That about did it for me, college-wise.

Meanwhile, I had been working nights and one evening my

big brother came by and made me leave work early. When I got down to the car my father was there, closer to tears than I ever saw him. He had been fired. An architect by choice, he returned to the profession after the Hollywood blacklist. But now, past 50, his background had caught up with him and he was now on the shit-list of L.A. architectural firms. It was pathetic to see a man, grow-ing old, forced out of the only work he knew and really liked (a habitual bad driver, he was always in or causing accidents as he redesigned the city in his mind, oblivious to the traffic around him), wrestle with the problem of what to do with the rest of his life. My mother, who had been working graveyard and swing shifts as a railroad stenographer, now became the sole breadwin-ner while my father was finding his way. He finally set up some dreck ersatz real-estate operation which, while profitable, he thor-oughly hates. All this happened while a retired general, running on batteries alone, held down the presidency of the country.

I drove up to the Bay Area for a few days to see what it looked like. That trip remains less than a blur in my memory except for one Great Event in my life. The first night in San Francisco, my traveling companion and I had about an hour or so before we were to meet some friends. We stepped into a broadway burlesque house called Ann's 440, where we provided the only audience for an unknown comic named Lenny Bruce. Lenny kept us there from nine until two in the morning and we came back the next night and the next, for almost a week. Back in L.A. we'd follow him from club to club. He was just developing his Religions Incorpo-rated, Boy in the Well, John Graham and the Airplane Explosion, Fatboy the Auto Salesman, and MCA Makes Hitler Dictator rou-tines. Lenny was the only man who really did make me laugh until it hurt, and after you saw him nobody else was really funny. It's like every actor is for me only second-best after seeing Olivier. I lost contact with him after a while, occasionally dropping by a club to hear him, but my little brother and he became very tight and even lived together for a while. A man who could say about Chicago and the Syndicate, "It's so corrupt, it's thrilling," he had more integrity than any other public personality of his time. Born Leonard Schneider, sprinkling his routines with Yiddishisms, he was the one true Christian I've ever seen. When he was finally killed, I wrote an obit entitled "How Not to Get Invited to a White House Dinner, or That Was No Cocksucker, That Was My Wife," which was rejected by two magazines because of the title. I figured that was obituary enough.

At the time when I first heard Lenny Bruce, George Gallup conducted a poll that showed that 58 percent of America's college students named *Mad* as their favorite magazine. It was a year when, three years after the CIA overthrow of the popularly elected government of Guatemala, J. Edgar Hoover began to warn about "crime in the streets" growing rampant. On my 17-year-old mind, Lenny had a profound political impact. He seemed to be the only one at the time who could distinguish an idea from a piece of shit and understood that the best means for disposal of the latter was to flush it down the toilet, or remove it from political office. For no good reason except that I first heard him there, it was Lenny Bruce that drew me to the Bay Area. I enrolled at Berkeley for the Fall 1958 semester.

four

*I can just see, having done arbitration in the
industrial scene, that the employers will love
this generation, that they are not going to
press many grievances . . . they are going to do
their jobs, they are going to be easy to handle.
There aren't going to be riots. There aren't going
to be revolutions. There aren't going to be many strikes.*
—CLARK KERR, 1959

The cardinal fact demonstrated by the old left-new left division is that McCarthyism worked.

Its anti-Communist ideological crusade in the churches, schools and media succeeded in eliminating a whole generation of radicals, resulting in a left movement today primarily composed of people over 50 and under 30. The McCarthyist campaign against "20 years of treason" (Richard Milhous Nixon's lovely characterization of the years preceding his rise to glory) couldn't help but leave its scars.

This absolute divorce of generations has forced new radicals to discover for themselves the years-old axioms accepted as basic truths by revolutionaries around the world. Because of their continuity and sense of tradition, European radical movements begin within a Marxist ideological framework and, from that base, mobilize campaigns against, say, U.S. aggression in Vietnam. For us, it has been necessary to reverse the process: to oppose the war, and from that opposition, discover the class nature of the system that perpetrates such wars.

Perhaps the most heinous result of the anti-Communist assaults was their erasing for the younger movements that essential tool for radicals, a sense of history. There are few who place the burden for the failures of the past on the faults of the "old left." (For those who may have missed the point these past few years, old left is usually a euphemism for the Communist Party and those who now or have in the past followed its leadership.) The prevailing view is that there really isn't an old left at all. The "new left" is the left. The cases of the Martinsville Seven, the Trenton Six, Willie McGee, the We Charge Genocide petition against police repression and for black liberation to the United Nations—all campaigns led by Communists, not in the glorious, near-mythical thirties, but in the late forties and early fifties—completely escape the knowledge of younger radicals.

When I came to Berkeley, my friends and I were of an age that didn't understand the agonies of the Depression or the glories of The War. Most had a narrow attitude toward working people. Taught by a collection of ex-radical, ex-Trotskyist and social-democratic social scientists, we were made to learn that workers were another "interest group" in our pluralist society, a "counter-vailing power" to balance that other power known as corporate business. The implication was that both had an equal voice in the affairs of the nation, that was how this most equitable of systems was programmed.

There was Big Labor and there was Big Business, and we shouldn't have any "romantic" notions that the working class was the agent of revolutionary change in industrial countries, such as our teachers held in days of yore. If anything the workers had been corrupted by the system, we were told by the most bought-off intelligentsia in human history. The affluent society had co-opted the working class, said our university, three-quarters of whose funds came from the Pentagon, Atomic Energy Commission, NASA, CIA and the Ford, Rockefeller, and Rand foundations.

Disillusioned former radicals praised the end of ideology. The young, however, needed one. The spiritual depression of most Berkeley academics was a reaction to the madness of the times. For myself, I came to radical politics, more than anything else, to make sense out of the madness. For ten years now, I have found politics more painful than exhilarating, more hard work than fun. I have personally enjoyed politics only occasionally. But for my sanity it is the most important element in my life, for it still makes sense out of the madness of the system that controls our lives.

Arriving in Berkeley the day before Fall 1958 registration, with housing near the campus at a premium, I checked into the first furnished room available, three blocks toward the Bay from school. A bed, desk, chair, and lamp are what qualified the room as "furnished" and the landlady, in moments of Christian charity, would offer me a hot plate on loan. My first six months at the university revolved around that oppressive little room, where I would lay for hours reading, with periodic excursions to a round of incredibly dull classes, a swing-shift job in a paint supplies warehouse, the local poolhall, and the City.

There were next to no politics to speak of, and to speak of politics was considered mundane by most, quaint by some. The University alumni magazine, writing about the period a few years later, held that, "The extreme poles of liberalism and conservatism are clearly unattractive to most students." And most academics searched for some middle ground between such extremes.

Arriving on the iron heels of McCarthyism, students feared to accept leaflets at university gates; petitions were a trap, and picket lines a dim memory from a best-forgotten decade. There had been occasional outbursts of protest a few years earlier. The "Green Feather" campaign, for one, began when an Indiana group sought to ban Robin Hood stories from the public schools. Sparked by the Communist-led Labor Youth League, thousands of students wore green feathers in protest of the times. But the League had been dissolved by 1957. More advanced universities in the country, like that at Berkeley, with a penchant for slumming, for tinkering with liberalism, set up "Hyde Park" areas, or held "Hyde Park Days." These little ghettos of free speech were the only spots where the U.S. Constitution was allowed on campus.

Meanwhile, in the southern states, a movement was taking shape which would shake the entire country. Since *Brown vs. Board of Education* in 1954, school desegregation was proceeding with all deliberate speed, a pace of about one percent a year. A few dozen counties still had no black voters registered, but this was more than compensated for by the fact that in a like number of counties white registration exceeded 100 percent. Black people were still barred from equal use of lunch counters, public toilets and other free world facilities. Emmett Louis Till and Charles Mack Parker were both lynched and fed to the Mississippi, their murderers unapprehended. Youth unemployment among blacks was upwards of 30 percent. And the White Citizens Councils, formed first in 1954, grew rapidly and rabidly. But when Rosa Parks refused to sit in the back of the bus in 1956, she touched off a 381-day bus boycott in Montgomery, the cradle of the confederacy, and there was no turning back. Case Number One for me that folks could, against all odds, organize to determine their own lives; that one could fight for justice, because the struggle itself gives meaning to one's life.

I recall Case Number Two for the most incongruous of reasons. An aficionado of football, I went to every Cal game in the only approximation I could make of school spirit. When "we" won the right to go to the Rose Bowl on New Year's Day against Iowa, I bought a number of tickets for scalping. Money in pockets, hung over from the night before, the game itself remains a blur, although I do recall that Cal lost miserably. But coming out of the stadium in Pasadena, I became the happiest fan in California when I saw the afternoon headlines: Batista Flees as Rebels March on Havana. They gave the lie to the argument that people were impotent to control their future. Whatever barriers we faced to political expression were not insurmountable.

A few years before I entered Berkeley, the state legislature played with the idea of a faculty loyalty oath. University administrators decided to preserve the autonomy of the university by proposing their own loyalty oath. Students and faculty members actively fought the oath, and many left when it was finally adopted, draining the radical spirit at the school. Sporadic incidents indicated that the oath had not eliminated dissent entirely. A campaign, supported by thousands, was mustered around the refusal of the University of Alabama to allow black co-ed Autherine Lucy to register. A petition campaign of similar proportions was waged for the first time against compulsory ROTC.

In 1957, a graduate student representative on the student government raised the issue of discriminatory clauses in fraternity and sorority constitutions. The government executive committee refused to act, and a slate of candidates organized to run for student office on the issue. In losing, they demonstrated by a high vote that a campus political party could be viable. Toward an Active Student Community (TASC) was founded and floundered through the spring and fall of 1957. A TASC member of student government, Mike Miller, resigned from the executive committee, announcing that he would run on a common platform with other candidates as a slate. Running officially as SLATE, they were barred from the ballot but reinstated after pressure. Red-baited for calling attention to discrimination in housing, low campus wages and denials of academic freedoms, the SLATE met electoral defeat while compiling 40 percent of the vote, and raising the total vote for student government elections from 3,000 in the spring to 4,700 by fall. Encouraged by the results, a founding convention was called for SLATE as a campus political party, and a party organ, *Cal Reporter*, established under the editorship of Hank Di Suvero, later to become a prominent radical lawyer in New York.

Early in the spring of 1959, I was leaving the campus with a couple of friends on our way for a beer on Telegraph Avenue. At Sather Gate, the south entrance to the school, a crowd was gathered to hear SLATE speakers on the current Berkeley city elections. The major issue was a proposed fair housing ordinance, which SLATE's housing committee was canvassing for in the university community. A ruling had just come down from the dean of students that SLATE could not campaign on campus because it was a city, not a university, issue. Not inconsequentially, the dean was a candidate at the time for city council, running against the antidiscrimination bill.

After three or four rally speakers, word came from the dean's office, not 50 yards away, that disciplinary measures might be taken against speakers violating his fiat. Without really thinking, I told my friends to wait a few minutes, and I mounted the platform just to give my name and address and to associate myself with the remarks of the previous speakers. I hadn't yet finished my 30-second statement, when I saw Danny and Richard, leaving the spot where they waited for me, come up on the platform themselves and do the same thing I had done. Fourteen others followed them. Within the next 24 hours, we were all called in to the dean's office to set the date for a disciplinary hearing; I had joined SLATE, as had Danny, and the two of us were appointed to head up grievance negotiations with Chancellor Glenn Seaborg. That was a full decade ago, and not a day has passed since that I have not been engaged.

That embryonic free speech movement led us to set up the first of many of what have come to be termed "front groups." The Student Civil Liberties Union, headed up by Aryay Lenske, another of the fourteen impromptu rally speakers, was immediately accepted by the ACLU as a student affiliate. We set up shop in the campus YMCA, Stiles Hall. This first *foco* was under the direction of Bob Walters, a wonderful man whose role in the early development of the Berkeley student movement was immense, and who later wrote a fictionalized account of those days, *Stacy Tower,* now available in paperback at your local Greyhound bus station.

Together with finding ourselves thrust into a movement, we also developed a new social life. I suppose this was a big factor in sustaining my political energies. Living in hibernation in my hovel for so many months had left me with a handful of acquaintances and fewer friends among a student body of 25,000. Within a week of the fair housing rally, we had organized an eating commune in Aryay's apartment, which had a stove but no refrigerator, but which was a couple of houses away from another member, who had a refrigerator but no stove. The poorest of us, a fifteen-year-old prodigy from New York, would make as his contribution a full supply of Coltrane and Miles records, which he had lifted. My own ante was a horrible 99-cents-a-gallon red Burgundy, El Capitan, which would light us up to proportions necessary to get us through the myriad meetings which we called. Perhaps the great irony of my life is choosing a passion that necessitates so many meetings, the most dreadful of all ways to pass time. To this day, 10,000 meetings later, I cannot get through one without becoming antsy. In 1959, however, El Capitan was enough to see us through. Either that, or margaritas from a dumpy little Mexican restaurant in downtown Oakland, Mexacali Rose, where we would luxuriate on my twice-monthly paycheck. Coming juiced to SLATE assemblies, we would contribute our quota of two or three outrageous statements, undoubtedly embarrassing the body thoroughly, and sleep out the duration.

As the semester was nearing its end, the House Committee on Un-American Activities announced from Washington its imminent arrival in our fair community to investigate the educational system out our way. One hundred and ten persons, mainly teachers, were served with subpoenas. Aryay and I were charged with the responsibility of organizing resistance to the committee. Danny, the son of a prominent Beverly Hills psychoanalyst, was to mobilize broad support, broad being a euphemism for the rich and renowned who were prepared to add their names to letterheads. Within a week, several thousand student signatures and hundreds of protests from community organizations and prominent individuals helped convince the committee that it best remain at home for a while. The subpoenas were quashed and we were granted a reprieve. For a year.

Student government elections were coming up. We were now a full-fledged political party, with an organization, a good deal of infamy, and an appeal: All other candidates ran as individuals, with no holding them to account, when their term is over, they can leave; a party, if it fails to hold to its promises, can always be voted out. In our case, a full slate was offered the voter, as ecumenical a collection as has ever run together: three graduate rep candidates, Carey McWilliams, Jr., son of *The Nation*'s editor, and our Von Clausewitz; Mike Gucovsky, an Eastern European refugee; and Marv Sternberg, an economics instructor who was one of the few bridges to whatever movement existed in the darkest McCarthy days; a number of undergraduate candidates, including Danny and Aryay, and Cindy Lembcke, then SLATE chairman.

David Armor, a SLATE member of the student government executive committee already, was chosen to run for student body president. David and his wife, Marilyn, SLATE's answer to Eddie and Debbie, had come to Berkeley from Victorville, a small Southern California desert town. They used to tell about how surprised they were in Berkeley upon meeting Jews for the first time; what they expected from Victorville was that all Jews wore black robes, beards, *yamulkes* and *payess*. Today a sociology professor at Harvard, David did not venture to San Francisco in his first three years at Berkeley.

A mobilization among fraternities and sororities to defeat SLATE produced the largest election turnout in the university's history. Amassing nine-tenths of the graduate student vote, David was elected president, and Cindy and the three graduate reps also won their seats. Administration response was swift; suddenly, graduate students were disenfranchised and ejected from the student government. The reason given for the action was that they had "voted" not to remain in the undergraduate student government. Actually no vote was ever taken. There had once been a registration poll that presented graduates with a series of alternatives on student government, although no alternative received a majority. No debate or discussion of the issues had taken place.

But this poll was used by the university administration to eliminate graduate support of SLATE.

Student elections, a microcosm of those in the outside world, gave us some indication of who really held power. And electoral politics, it seemed, only reflected the real political situation. We could use them to mobilize, to organize, to educate, but we could not depend on them as an instrument for change. They might at times be used to build a democratic movement, but elections could never be a goal for us, as long as the present power relationship held. At best, they could be used to dispel illusions in a false democratic process. I think that from that election on, we never really did see student elections as anything more than a medium for our reaching students. Organizing movement around issues became our central task; the administration, and the system it represents, our main enemy.

Clark Kerr, the university president, understood this every bit as well as we were coming to, and issued the first "Kerr directives." Given the temper of the period, the issues around which we organized, indeed that we organized at all, made us radical: opposition to nuclear tests, low-cost housing for married students, medical care for dependents, opposition to state right-to-work legislation. That we considered some accomplishments as victories tells something about the mood of Berkeley, vintage 1959: the right to pass out leaflets during elections, the right to invite controversial speakers to campus, increased minimum student wage from 90 cents to $1.30 an hour. Even these petty reforms, and the fact that we were getting increasing support, indicated to the administrators that something must be done. The first Kerr directive forbade recognized campus groups from taking stands on "off-campus religious, economic, international or other issues of the time." On the face of it unconstitutional, not to say ridiculous, this directive from the leading ideologist of higher education in the nation brought a barrage of protests and threatened lawsuits.

After a major campaign, Kerr modified his ruling so that campus groups still were not "allowed" to take stands on outside issues, but individuals who were members of such groups could. Looking back from a decade's distance, it seems incredible that the largest university in the world could be so provincial and stupidly reactionary. In any case, that was the beginning of a career for Clark Kerr that finds him "off-campus" today.

The Pentagon had as much influence in university life then as today, but had not yet thought to apply the domino theory to domestic politics. Within a year of Armor's election, and after a dozen visits by some of us to other campuses, the country was anagrammed with campus political parties: PLATFORM at UCLA, PROGRESS at Oregon State, TASC and SPUR at San Jose State, Progressive Students League at Oberlin, ACTION at Columbia, FOCUS at Reed, SCOPE at San Francisco State, POLIT at Chicago. We had also helped begin an organization of young workers, STEP, in the Bay Area. We decided to hold the first SLATE summer conference at Mt. Madonna, California, attended by students from some 40 campuses. One, a student editor from Ann Arbor named Tom Hayden, stayed the summer, and afterwards returned to the University of Michigan to form a party called VOICE. Eric Hobsbawm, the British Marxist historian, on sabbatical at Stanford, came to the conference as an observer and wrote his observations for the *New Statesman,* focusing international attention for the first time on the new North American student movement.

Of course, we were still but a relatively small band. Most students were little more than half through their Rip Van Winkle slumber of 20 years. Hayden recalled asking a girl on the verge of graduation what her most valuable educational experience had been, and her answer: "The experience of meeting so many different kinds of people and becoming aware of all the different viewpoints there are." Of the "different viewpoints," she subscribed to none. Commented Tom: "Her answer, I think, is typical on college campuses and seems to be the 20th century product of the celebrated system of liberal or general education. What is remarkable about the statement is its apparent enthusiasm without deep involvement. The girl had become aware of something, but her life had not been changed. She had become conscious of the living world of people and ideas but made no existential commitment to either."

For us who had become committed, ideological disagreements arose. The question of racism, rampant at the university and a problem even within our ranks, was a constant difficulty. The city of Berkeley was one-third black, and the ghetto was so clearly segregated from the white community, an alert twelve-year-old could make out the town's Mason-Dixon line on a street map. Yet scarcely 100 black students, less than half of one percent of the total student body, went to the university. While SLATE had committees on discrimination in housing and employment, an advanced position for most college students at the time, most of its members were aloof from the problem.

The biggest division in SLATE existed between those who wished it to become ideological and those that contended it should remain what they called "issues-oriented." In part, the division was artificial. Only one defined ideological group operated in the organization: the Young Peoples Socialist League (YPSL), the youth-wing of the Socialist Party. YPSL (which Paul Krassner remarked reminded him of a Jewish kid in Crown Heights: "Ypsl! Ypsl! Come on in the house, supper's ready.") had a very talented local *guru* named Bogden Denitch, and every so often it would bring its New York heavyweights, Mike Harrington and Norman Thomas, to the West Coast. (The young Trotskyist sect for the most part stayed away from SLATE.)

Problems arose when YPSL would press SLATE to take anti-Communist positions. Holding to its "third camp" stance, that the socialist camp and the United States were equally guilty for the cold war, YPSL always worked to convince SLATE that it should adopt a similar position. Actually, this outlook was dominant in the peace and student movements across the country and remained so for a few years afterward. It was in fact the view subscribed to by the infant Students for a Democratic Society, a view that began to deteriorate at Playa Giron and was finally bombed to smithereens by LBJ when he sent his air force into the Democratic Republic of Vietnam.

Those of us who rejected the anti-Communism of YPSL were not necessarily opposed to developing an ideology. But we had none at the time, we were only then beginning to grow as an organization, and in bidding for time, clung to the "issues" orientation. We were perhaps the only active non-anti-Communists of our generation. Rejecting the cold war, we held that to make politics legitimate once again in the United States then we had to make radical politics legitimate. We demanded the right to cooperate with whomever we wished, free of oaths and disclaimers. If others wanted anti-Communist organizations, heaven knew there were enough of those around. Of course, this brought the combined wrath of cold war apologists such as Seymour Martin Lipset, Robert Pickus, Lewis Feuer and others down upon our unprotected craniums.

And it focused with ever greater precision and intensity university administration attacks on SLATE. When the *Daily Californian* endorsed SLATE candidate Michael Tigar for student body president following Armor's term of office, the anti-SLATE student government maneuvered to completely emasculate the campus paper. The staff quit in protest hours before they were fired de facto. The student government executive committee, with the aid of "volunteers" and paid professionals, continued turning out the paper while the old staff unsuccessfully launched a private paper. The *Daily Californian* staggered through the year, no less political than previously, but with an editor who climaxed his career by supporting the FLN in Algeria and Moral Re-Armament, both in the same week and with the same sophomoric passion. That same campus election, which brought 7,500 undergraduates to the polls, defeated the SLATE candidates by a few hundred votes on the slogan "America si, Tigar no!"

Another campus group we helped to organize, Students for Racial Equality, was always stifled by administration fiats. The only student political organization with a substantial number of black students, SRE was originally formed to raise scholarship money for sit-in students expelled by Southern universities, but expanded its activities to campaign for aid to the struggle in the Tennessee counties of Fayette and Haywood. After we had held a successful fund-raising concert with the Oscar Peterson Trio and the Cannonball Adderly Quintet, the administration said we could not hold another, that in fact we were a wing of the student government and had no independent existence. This pretext sprung from the fact that Dan Greenson, a SLATE member of student government, had been instrumental in organizing SRE.

About the same time, an invitation to Malcolm X to come to Cal to speak on the Nation of Islam was denied permission by the university because Malcolm was "inflammatory" and further, that a clause in the state constitution forbade state university facilities from being used for religious purposes. That same year had seen Rev. Roy Nichols of the Berkeley Board of Education, Billy Graham, and Rabbi Fine address university audiences. Indeed, Bishop James Pike spoke on campus the very afternoon Malcolm had originally been scheduled.

Also that semester, several NAACP members and people from the sociology department picketed the university employment service for allowing airlines which discriminated in hiring policies to recruit new employees on the campus. The administration remonstrated with the pickets because its policy forbade on-campus picketing. Of course, it lacked a policy forbidding the use of its facilities for discriminatory hiring by private industry.

University authorities came at us from all angles. SLATE's faculty advisor, one of at most a dozen professors friendly to student insurgents, an exceptional man named Richard Drinnon, was denied tenure on grounds of "insufficient publication," although University of Chicago Press had just announced the forthcoming publication of his biography of the anarchist, Emma Goldman. Drinnon was much more than an advisor: he became a leader in the Chessman campaign and the struggle against HUAC; and he was a persistent pain in the collective ass of the academic senate, because if he was willing to risk the loss of all the dubious rewards of Berkeley faculty status, why not they.

But the university's administration had no corner on repression. State legislators, fraternity politicians, the local press corps, and an assortment of budding Fascist groups all vied with one another in outrageous attacks on our rather puny ranks. After our sponsoring Herbert Aptheker and anti-HUAC organizer Frank Wilkinson to speak on campus (Wilkinson's talk sparked bomb threats, a rightist march on the state capital, and an audience of 8,000), a group was formed calling itself Students Associated Against Totalitarianism. SAAT published, first in mimeographed form and later in slick print, a hate sheet called *Tocsin*. This latter-day aspirant to the mantle of *Red Channels* had a particular lust for SLATE, but was put out of business finally with a threat of a lawsuit. The whole dreary attack was climaxed when a local psychopath, with notions of firing the opening shot of World War III, went hunting for Professor Drinnon, found poet-professor Tom Parkinson instead, and blew half of Parkinson's face off, killing a visiting graduate student in the process.

Graduation Day has each time been a day of surprises for me. Barred from speaking at my junior high school commencement, expelled from high school the day I was sent forth into the adult world, my last day as a student at the university had much deeper significance. I was home in bed as President Kerr told those participating in the ceremonies, regarding the new student movement: "Their basic and intensely-felt concerns for social equality and intellectual liberty are not out of line with either the present national temper or with our fundamental American heritage . . . [They reflect] the continuing American vision of a free society of free men. . . . We should be, and we are proud to be associated with today's students. We should preserve for them and for those who will follow them a university environment where they can be free to hear and to read, to talk and to act, within the bounds of responsibility and respect for orderly procedures."

Chairman of SLATE at the time, I was on the phone with an Associated Press reporter, even as Kerr spoke, who had called to tell me that SLATE had been suspended from campus, and did I have a statement. The San Francisco *News-Call Bulletin* the next day ran a banner headline: U.C. OUSTS LIBERAL CLUB—As Freedom is Defended. The story began, "SLATE, the University of California's liberal student group was banned from the Berkeley campus by university officials today—Commencement Day—just a few hours before Governor Brown, UC President Clark Kerr and student speakers hailed academic freedom. . . ."

five

*If people bring so much courage to this world
the world has to kill them to break them, so
of course it kills them. . . . It kills the very
good and the very gentle and the very brave
impartially. If you are none of these you can
be sure it will kill you too but there will be
no special hurry.*
   —ERNEST HEMINGWAY, A Farewell to Arms

*Clevinger recoiled from their hatred as though
from a blinding light. These three men who
hated him spoke his language and wore his uniform, but he saw their loveless faces set immu-
table into cramped, mean lines of hostility and
understood instantly that nowhere in the world,
not in all the fascist tanks or planes or sub-
marines, not in the bunkers behind the machine
guns or mortars or behind the blowing flame
throwers, not even among all the expert gunners
of the crack Hermann Goering Anti-aircraft Division or among the grisly connivers in all the
beer halls in Munich and everywhere else, were
there men who hated him more.*
   —Catch 22

Categorizing is always an intellectually dangerous pastime, but the savants who first dreamed up the concept of the "civilized world" could not have known just how tortuous a path they were treading. "Free world" now updates the earlier category, but both have been used to denote the advanced industrial nations of the West. How's this for a phenomenal box score credited to contemporary Western civilization: 40 million exterminated in World War II, over half "barbaric" Russians, at the hands of the Germany of Goethe and Bach; 300,000 lives snuffed out in minutes at Hiroshima and Nagasaki by the current front runner in free worlddom; five million peasants killed since the War in the course of intervention by the imperial powers—150,000 in Madagascar by the French, a quarter of a million in Kenya by the British, one million in Algeria by the French, close to two million in Vietnam by the French and North Americans, and hundreds of thousands more from Laos to Angola to Guatemala. Spokesmen for these "free world" powers today lament "the breakdown of law and order" and "crime in the streets, where a body can't be safe these days."

The alienation of citizens from the political process is at once a major cause and major effect of this commitment to organized mass violence. However, for myself, the single most alienating act of this nation, was the legal murder of one man, Caryl Chessman. For many years it has been known that capital punishment neither reforms the offender nor helps the victim; it doesn't even deter others from committing crime. As former California Governor Edmund Brown admitted: "The death penalty has been a gross failure. Beyond its horror and incivility, it has neither protected the innocent nor deterred the wicked. The recurrent spectacle of publicly sanctioned killing has cheapened human life and dignity without the redeeming grace which comes from justice meted out swiftly, evenly, humanely."

Brown, who is perhaps the single man most responsible for Chessman's murder, has indicated the nature of justice in these United States and against whom the death penalty is administered: "No matter how efficient and fair the death penalty may seem in theory, in actual practice in California as elsewhere it is primarily inflicted upon the weak, the poor, the ignorant, and against racial minorities. . . . In the experience of former wardens Lewis Lawes of Sing Sing and Clinton P. Duffy of San Quentin, seldom are those with funds or prestige convicted of capital offenses, and even more seldom are they executed.

"As shocking as may be the statistics in our deep South (twelve Southern states have the highest homicide rate) where the most extensive use of the death penalty is made and against the most defenseless and downtrodden of the population, the Negroes, let it be remembered too that in California, in the fifteen-year period ending in 1953, covering 110 executions, 30 percent were of Mexicans and Negroes, more than double the combined population percentages of these two groups at the time. Indeed, only last year, 1959, out of 48 executions in the United States, 21 only were whites, while 27 were Negroes."

When one combines these figures with the knowledge that virtually all blacks sent to their death or to prison go on the findings of all-white and majority-white juries, respect must be granted the demand of the Black Panther Party that black prisoners be released because they have been denied their constitutional guarantee of trial by peers. In fact, all systems of justice will reflect the economic-political system that prevails. A racist society will have racist justice, and a system where wealth prevails and profit is made by a few of the many, will administer law on the same basis.

Deaths as punishment must be distinguished from deaths, including civil deaths, resulting from war. That is, the Tories executed by the Revolutionary Army following the victory of the thirteen American Colonies against England, or the execution of

Batista's torturers by the Cuban revolutionary government upon its ascension to power, can be seen as the continuation of those wars. But for a peacetime government, all available evidence demonstrates that the death penalty neither reforms nor deters. Rather, capital punishment, the legal means of taking life from an accused, is the ultimate admission that a society is unable to reform its members.

California has always had something of a minority complex, being until recently second to Texas in size, and to New York in numbers. But, thinking big, its state legislatures have listed six capital offenses in addition to treason against the state: first-degree murder, kidnapping, train wrecking, perjury in a capital trial resulting in the execution of an innocent person, sabotage, and assault by a life prisoner.

Caryl Chessman, the most famous prisoner of his time, was sent to San Quentin's Death Row on technical charges of kidnapping arising from armed robberies in which female victims were sexually molested. Continually depicted by the press as a "convicted rapist-killer," this basic inaccuracy—Chessman, even if guilty as charged, neither raped nor killed anyone—became a fantasy-reality by virtue of constant repetition. Chessman was accused of being Los Angeles' "Red Light Bandit," so named because of a police light used to frighten the couples he robbed in L.A.'s lover's lane, Mulholland Drive. Victimized by the California press, Chessman's most inflammatory alleged deed was driving one victim, a seventeen-year-old girl, crazy by his torment. In fact, the girl had a history of psychotic behavior before the crime, and did not flip out until two years after. The news stories calling the "Red Light Bandit" a "kidnap-rapist" were equally inaccurate. The crimes committed were construed as kidnappings under a vaguely-worded law, amended three years later in 1951, that defined kidnap as a movement of a robbery victim even one inch. Such a law, one critic pointed out, could have been used to send every heist man in the state to the gas chamber. All the press, including the Los Angeles paper of record. the *Times*, described Chessman's alleged sex offenses as "unprintable," "unnatural" and "indescribable." This "unnatural" act was having the victim perform fellatio, a practice engaged in by over 60 percent of Dr. Alfred Kinsey's sampling. But it was not rape, in any case.

Chessman's first fifteen years of life were marked by poverty and disease, nearly dying of diphtheria and later, at age ten, of encephalitis. His mother was crippled by a traffic accident, and his father, beset by business failures in the Depression, twice attempted suicide. Caryl, preceding me at L.A.'s John Marshall High School by 20 years, began a life of crime by stealing food so his parents would not have to accept relief packages. He spent the next seventeen of his 23 years behind bars, more than the state average for convicted murderers. Twelve years on Death Row, he spent 22 hours a day in a concrete cubicle too narrow for him to stretch his arms. And he had to prepare himself for hydrocyanic death nine different times, certainly the record for contemporary refined torture.

Cops, press and prosecutors all viewed Chessman's exercising his constitutional right of due process as "quibbling over legal loopholes." After nine years on Death Row, during which three wardens had come and gone at San Quentin, the U.S. Supreme Court opined that he had "never had his day in court upon the controversial issues of fact and law involved in the settlement of the record upon which his conviction was affirmed." The court also declared the state had "violated [his] constitutional right to procedural due process" when it denied him permission to be his own attorney in 1949, when the record of the trial was certified as accurate. The original court reporter died of a heart attack before he had transcribed more than a-third of his notes. Deputy D.A. J. Miller Leavy of Los Angeles appointed a substitute court reporter to finish the job. The new reporter, coincidentally a relative of

D.A. Leavy, made more than 2,000 errors in the course of his job. Chessman elicited from the substitute at least 40 admissions of failure to transcribe the dead stenographer's symbols and 30 admissions that he [the substitute] had changed or added symbols.

Chessman's great crimes were being proud and unrepentant. Accused of being "remorseless," he would not plead for mercy nor ask forgiveness; he denied up to his death his guilt in the Red Light crimes. He was contrite about his early life of violence, but regarding his refusal to ask for clemency in the alleged capital offenses, he said, "For almost twelve years I've been fighting for a new trial so I can prove my innocence. The court action is still going on. While it continues, it would be foolhardy of me to prejudice my case by seeking mercy as if I were guilty."

In those twelve years, he more than proved his usefulness to society by his writings, four full works of which were printed, much to the embarrassment of the authorities. Exposing the weakness of the judicial and penological systems, he acquired a reputation as one of the finest appeals lawyers in the country. He pioneered educational work on behalf of illiterate convicts, gave legal assistance and wrote briefs for other condemned men. It was his fuck-you stance toward the authorities that made them kill him. Following a celebrated tradition of becoming a convict-author, Chessman was a deserved heir to others, like Marco Polo, Cervantes, St. Paul, Defoe, Balzac, Oscar Wilde, Gorky, O. Henry, Dostoevsky, Gramsci, Dmitroff, Gandhi, and Bertrand Russell; and to other condemned prisoners like Villon, Savonarola, Sir Walter Raleigh and Thomas More. What was unique about Caryl Chessman was that he defied the authorities by his writings. Ordered to cease writing after his first book became a bestseller, his other manuscripts were confiscated. Subsequent books were smuggled out of San Quentin.

Three things drew me to the Chessman case: my own repugnance to the press hysteria which, from personal experience, I knew to be deceitful; respect and admiration for Chessman's courage; and the cruelty exhibited by the authorities, first and foremost Governor Brown. Late in October 1959, Brown denied clemency just days before Chessman's seventh execution date on the specious ground that the prisoner hadn't evidenced repentance, difficult by any standards for one who maintains his innocence. The Governor, an admitted advocate of abolition of capital punishment, could never summon up the courage to save the celebrated convict's life. Later claims that his hands were tied had little validity inasmuch as he himself had done the tying. The October execution was postponed to allow for another Supreme Court appeal. With the appeal's denial, a new date for the execution was set: February 19, 1960.

Some friends and I got together to form a committee to save Chessman and abolish the death penalty. Traveling around the state gathering petition signatures, we began mounting a drive that soon corresponded to those already operating at full speed in Uruguay, Italy, Sweden, and dozens of other countries. From the city of São Paulo, Brazil, alone, some two million signatures were gathered. But Brown continually refused to see us. On February 17, two days before the execution was to take place, a friendly faculty member tipped us off that Brown was to speak that noon at a conference in San Francisco's Fairmont Hotel. Three of us rushed over, bundles of signed petitions in hand, to crash the party. One of our impromptu delegation, a black student, was, quite unintentionally, and very much at random, chosen to make the presentation. Alerting the press to our plans, they gathered as the Governor emerged from the dais. As our friend rushed up, Brown, spotting him and figuring to receive another NAACP accolade, he, much to our surprise and consternation, turned on his pol grin, which lasted maybe two seconds before he realized what had happened. The photograph that flashed over the airwaves that night showed the good guv looking like he'd just farted in church.

Two nights later, hundreds of us gathered at the gates of the prison as the hour of doom approached. Word came that Brown had granted a 60-day reprieve to Chessman on the grounds that it would save President Eisenhower embarrassment during his impending tour of Latin America. Without sufficient good grace to make the reprieve on the merits of the case, the Governor took honors in the *chutzpah* sweepstakes.

Our protests resumed again. Support from celebrities like Marlon Brando, Shirley McLaine and Steve Allen was solicited. Delegation after delegation visited the Governor's Mansion in Sacramento; thousands upon thousands marched in the streets. But Ike was back in his den, and the execution would proceed as scheduled this ninth, and final, time. Simultaneous demonstrations on the eve of the murder were maintained at the prison gate, and the state capital 90 miles to the north. We waited in silence, chilled by the winds blowing off the bay.

It was now eleven years and 305 days since Caryl Chessman was first moved to Death Row, and the cruel and unusual punishment begun. Were Governor Brown to stay the execution another thirty days, the prisoner would have won his right to live. Twenty-eight days later a replacement was to be made on the state supreme court, and the new appointee had already announced he would vote for commutation, tipping the delicate balance between life and death. But the Governor, once again playing to the press gallery, said the idea of a stay was "repugnant" to him because he felt that the executive branch should not influence decisions of the judiciary. Another last-minute appeal failed when Chessman's attorneys insisted that the state penal code mandates the Adult Authority to make recommendations to the governor concerning clemency applications on behalf of men with two or more prior convictions, and the Authority had not yet acted in this case. The judge, who said he would grant a stay, ordered his secretary to call the warden. The secretary then misdialed the telephone, which proved fatal.

When she reached the prison finally, it was too late. The physician had harnessed the stethoscope across the condemned man's chest, its black tube hanging like an obscene umbilical cord. Chessman had walked shoeless through the green door of the octagonal extermination chamber, and braces were strapped around his stomach, arms and legs. The black tube was connected and the physician outside the chamber adjusted his stethoscope. The army of witnesses was all present and accounted for. As the prisoner himself wrote in his last letter: "The California executioner keeps banker's hours. He never kills before ten o'clock in the morning, never after four in the afternoon." His last conversation had been with the warden, who later reported, "He asked me to specifically state that he was not the Red Light Bandit! He felt that the end was near and he hoped he had contributed toward the end of capital punishment."

Caryl Chessman, a man who had never taken the life of another, wrote five years earlier in his book, *The Face of Justice:* "Roughly nine minutes, once the gas is generated, is the time it will take to kill me." He hit it close. The last guard emerged from the cyanide cage, sealed the door, and at 10:03¼ A.M. acid gurgled into the well under the chair; the bag of cyanide dropped into the acid to produce the deadly hydrocyanic acid gas. Gasping and convulsing against the straps, his head snapped up, then down, then up again. Finally he slumped forward, and at 10:12 was officially pronounced dead. Chessman's last conscious act was to give the thumbs-up salute as he died with as much dignity as a man can muster when gassed in the same way that society disposes of stray dogs.

Opponents of capital punishment have often contended that if the judge and jury could be present for the execution, the practice would soon be ended. Others have used the same logic to urge televised live coverage. My own thinking is that in these United States, such coverage might well be a boon to pay TV. The executioner at San Quentin has never had difficulty getting enough eyewitnesses, and the cases are few and far between of families turning off the six o'clock news during dinner because the Vietnam War was causing indigestion.

Eighteen hours before his death, Caryl Chessman penned his last letter: "I did want to live. I believed passionately that I could make a meaningful contribution to both literature and my society with my writings. I was determined to repay those people from many nations who spoke out for me, who believed in Caryl Chessman as a human being. It would have given me great satisfaction and a sense of purpose to have survived to vindicate their compassionate judgement.

"But a harsh fate, wearing judicial robes, has decreed death in a small octagonal room painted green. . . .

"I shall have been told, 'It's time'—time to take those few short steps, time to be strapped down in a straight-backed metal chair, time to be stared at by other men and women come to witness how the sovereign State of California snuffs out human life in the name of justice, time to smell the synthetic odor of peach blossoms, time to inhale and gag and have consciousness recede into an eternal black void. . . .

"Facing death, I say this again emphatically and without qualification: I was not Southern California's infamous Red Light Bandit. California convicted the wrong man. And it stubbornly refused to admit the possibility of its error, much less correct it. . . .

"In my own way, I have done all in my power to focus attention on this problem, to make the world aware of Death Rows and execution chambers. I regard myself as neither hero nor martyr. On the contrary, I am a confessed fool who is keenly aware of the nature and quality of the folly of his earlier rebellious years. I learned too late and only after coming to Death Row that each of us ever must be aware of the brotherhood of man and the responsibility we individually bear to act responsibly in translating this vital concept into the reality of everyday life. Circumstances may compel us to become our brother's keeper; I think we destroy something in ourselves when we become his executioner."

Compare the dignity of Caryl Chessman to the behavior of the Governor of California, or to Deputy D. A. Leavy of Los Angeles, who could say the day after the execution: "What did they expect us to do—give him a prize—a reward? I slept pretty good last night."

Chessman was no saint, but he fought for his life with the pride worthy of a hero. He became great in the shadow of death, and might have made profound contributions had lesser men equaled his courage by letting him live. His own attorney, George Davis, made this assessment: "Perhaps his greatest flaw, his greatest lack of character, was his unrelenting unwillingness to believe in something greater and bigger than himself. He almost prided himself on the fact that he remained an agnostic to the end." Asked what other inmates felt about Chessman as the hour of execution neared, one veteran member of the prison staff answered: "They liked Chessman—not because they know him, but because he bucked the system. They hate the system."

Which comes closer than any other explanation I've heard as to why Caryl Chessman had to die. Those who believe that justice is perfectly served by the dark chemistry contrived at San Quentin might ponder the words of Professor Christian Bay, a Norwegian lawyer who helped lead the fight for Chessman's life: "The death penalty in fact does deter the criminal, not from committing his crimes . . . but from standing up for his constitutional rights to fair treatment by the police and to a fair trial. The existence of the death penalty eases the task of obtaining convictions for noncapital offenses; it makes possible innumerable 'deals' that make the job of police officials easier and their record of obtained convictions more impressive. Also, and this is just one aspect of the same situation, the fear of the gas chamber has made many an accomplice in capital crimes turn State's witness in order to save his own neck at the expense of the lives of his comrades. All this may help the morale of the police, but scarcely the cause of justice or the protection of the innocent."

Outside San Quentin it was a lovely seductive spring day, the sailboats at 10:00 A.M. already filling the horizon of the bay. No synthetic peach blossoms here, but the scent of new shrubbery filling the hills of Marin. Perhaps a thousand of us awaited the news, as a couple dozen corpsmen from a local air force base taunted us with jeers and calls to "kill the sex fiend." A few of our number briefly sat down in a futile attempt to keep the hearse from entering the prison, but they were quickly arrested. When word came that Caryl Chessman was now dead, I started to cry, the first time I'd done so in nearly four years. All around me people were sobbing. Then a local Hearst photographer began to take pictures of the tearful mass. Abusing the woman next to me who was trying to shield herself from his lens, he kept pursuing her until I moved in to tell him to stop. When he continued, I smashed his camera and told him to get his ass out of sight, when Professor Bay stopped me. That is the sum total of violence I ever engaged in in all my time as a university student. And I have only shed tears twice since over politics: on Election Day 1960 at the thought that people had so little to vote about with Kennedy and Nixon presented to them as options; and a year later, when under the leadership of that election's victor, the Central Intelligence Agency assassinated Patrice Lumumba.

That day at San Quentin began for real my hatred for this system that governs us. The death penalty remains for those who are, in the words of Murray Kempton, amateurs without property.

In June 1964, Winston Moseley was convicted of murdering Kitty Genovese in Queens, N.Y., stabbing her fifteen times on the street while her screams for help went unheeded by the 38 persons who heard them. New screams were heard at the trial—cheers and applause from the 100 spectators as they heard the jury prescribe death in the electric chair. The judge, J. Irwin Shapiro, thanked the jurors for rendering "a signal service for justice," and told them: "Although I do not believe in capital punishment, when I see a monster like this I wouldn't hesitate to pull the switch on him myself."

It is the double-think of the Judges Shapiro and Governors Brown that has led us to the point where Ahmed Evans, a black man, is sentenced to die in Cleveland for defending himself against police assault, and James Earl Ray is spared his life for killing Dr. King. And to the day when the system incarcerates Muhammed Ali and Huey P. Newton, while sending Lester Maddox, Ronald Reagan and Nelson Rockefeller to their governors' mansions.

six

Disillusioned words like bullets bark
As human Gods aim for their mark
Made everything from toy guns that spark
To flesh colored Christs that glow in the dark
It's easy to see without lookin' too far
That not much
Is really sacred

While preachers preach of evil fates
Teachers teach that knowledge waits
Can lead to hundred dollar plates
Goodness hides behind its gates
But even the president of the United States
Sometimes must have
To stand naked.

—BOB DYLAN

Racism, like the deity, works in strange and mysterious ways. When the call for black power arose in 1966, many whites of good conscience and morality were shocked to find that the black liberation movement was not organized to give them a sense of purpose. Since the initial hurt reaction at the notion that blacks wished to run their own movement, an easy accommodation has taken place. Completely ignoring the responsibility of whites to combat racism where they are at, most movement whites have decided that racism is an issue to be left to blacks ("that's how they want it"), while other questions, like peace, remain the providence of whites.

Black communities are facing a furious police offensive of daily beatings, frame-ups and assassinations. When a nineteen-year-old student nurse is beaten, tortured and framed on a murder conspiracy charge by New York police, because she is black and a Panther, there is silence in the white population. But that same population is thrown into pandemonium by a fourteen-year-old poet and a seventeen-year-old high school senior's thesis, when their works are read over listener-supported FM radio, and preface a Metropolitan Museum of Art catalog. White folks become unhinged at the sight of black Cornell students with guns, even when they fire nary a bullet. But no agonized cries of protest are heard a month later, also in the spring of 1969, when *The N. Y. Times* reports from Florence, South Carolina, that: "Nine state troopers were acquitted today of Federal charges that they violated the civil rights of three Negro teenagers they killed and 27 others they wounded in a burst of shotgun and pistol fire on a college campus last year. . . . The government said that the troopers had used excessive force and voided any claim of self-defense by pouring round after round of gunfire into the retreating students. The government's testimony showed that 28 of the 30 persons wounded that night had been shot in the side or the back." And did anyone hear other than sounds of silence over the acquittal of the Algiers Motel murderer, a white Detroit cop, from Ted Kennedy or Richard Nixon, from Gene McCarthy or J. Edgar Hoover, all of whom from their different vantage points wax indignant about "black extremists."

What Dr. DuBois said over 60 years ago still holds: the color question is the question of the 20th century. And the odds are better than even against the 21st, if that question is not answered. Black liberation remains central to any progress in this country. And anybody who believes that it is possible to build a mass united movement on any other issue in these United States, in this day and age, without directly taking on the question of racist oppression, is foolishly delusioned.

Anybody at all familiar with the movement today of course attributes its beginnings to the Southern Freedom Movement. The symbolic significance of Rosa Parks, triply exploited and oppressed as a black, a woman and a worker, sparking the Montgomery boycott speaks volumes for future developments. At every point since that time, black people have led the way in what *Newsweek* has called the Second American Revolution. There is a natural progression from the four black students in Greensboro who first refused to leave the "whites only" lunch counter in 1960, to the brothers in Los Angeles five years later who consciously emulated their Vietnamese contemporaries by firing on police helicopters vamping on Watts from the sky.

The execution of Caryl Chessman that May 2nd of 1960 had been preceded three months earlier by the wave of lunch counter sit-ins throughout the South. Ten days after the siege ended on the one-man occupied country that was Chessman, the Student Nonviolent Coordinating Committee was formed at Atlanta University. The sympathy picket demonstrations at Northern branches of Woolworth's represented the first real forays into the noncampus communities. The affinity of our fledgling student movement for the black liberation movement was thereafter inexorably bound. The rise of the Nation of Islam and its most eloquent and dynamic spokesman, Malcolm X Shabazz, began to excite our interest. When we organized the Northern California chapter of Fair Play for Cuba, our first speaking tour featured then North Carolina NAACP leader Robert Williams. The history of what has followed is more than a little familiar to the nation.

A hundred other flowers bloomed as well that spring. The Agricultural Workers Organizing Committee (AWOC) was sowing the seeds of the present farm workers union, and we set up a student affiliate, raising food and clothing for striking workers, and helping man union centers in Tracy and Stockton. Another major activity was our campaign against compulsory Reserve Officers Training Corps on the campus. This had initially been an issue raised by SLATE, but now, in coordination with the other campuses of the university, we were able to gather several thousand petition signatures. When that failed, we organized the first picket line in decades on a California campus. By today's standards pretty tame fare, that picket line brought the prunes of wrath down on our heads. The state un-American committee and its elder sibling in Washington vied with one another in pointing out the dangerous implications of this extremist action. While of course they were for a free marketplace of ideas, there was no booth available for us to peddle this subversive shit. It was one thing to discuss; that is the rule of reason. But when one starts to mount picket lines, clearly the rule of passion presides. When eighteen-year-old Fred Moore, son of an Air Force officer, was assigned Kierkegaard and Camus in freshman required courses, he decided he was a pacifist, refused to participate in ROTC, and went on a week-long hunger strike on the steps of the administration building. Thousands of students came to his support and the university, seeing where the movement was heading, a year later let the rule of reason persuade it to allow the ROTC to become voluntary.

An embryo was taking shape that would grow to become a massive antiwar movement. In January 1960, Herman Kahn dropped his token into the terror machine and read aloud the saying it produced: "We must be able both to stand up to the threat of fighting a war and to credibly threaten to initiate one." On May Day, the day before the Chessman execution, Gary Powers' U-2 was blasted from the sky over the Soviet Union, and President Ike compounded the disaster with lies and double-lies. The incident caused a few drops of righteous indignation to fall from the brows of the more hardy editorial writers. But it also produced the greatest California boom since the gold strike more than a century earlier. We now had bomb shelters. Folks stocked up on canned goods and condensed milk, reconverted their basements and cellars, and waited with shotguns in hand. Even jolly old Santa would get his if he tried sneaking down the chimney that Christmas. With signs above their army surplus cots reading "Be it ever so humble, there's no place like home," neighbors heeded their preachers' warnings to shoot each other on sight. Citizens, as Damon Runyon called them, screamed all the way to the banks to arrange E-Z credit terms for downpayments on their shelters. Untold millions were made on the swindle, put over on this most democratic of nations by her public servants in Washington and the state houses. A happy symbolic ending to the boom came when AP wirephotos flashed a picture across the news media of Dr. Edward Teller's $50,000 shelter, washed away in one of Southern California's annual mud slides.

Other free world nations were having their troubles. On March 19th, in Sharpeville, South Africa, police massacred a peaceful assembly of several thousand protesting the domestic passport laws. Sixty-seven nonviolent demonstrators were killed and 200 wounded. The present armed struggle raging across Southern Africa against the fascist and colonial regimes can be traced back directly to the Sharpeville atrocity. In Berkeley, a fund drive was organized to aid the surviving victims. This was the first act of solidarity with a foreign movement on our part. We began to link up our cause with theirs as we came to understand a common enemy. Within months, student-led demonstrations brought to an end the Rhee and Menderes dictatorships in Korea and Turkey, and kept President Eisenhower from going to Tokyo to sign the so-called U.S.-Japan Security Treaty, giving the former military hegemony over the latter.

On May 14, 1960, a news photo flashed around the world, giving notice that North American students were to take their rightful place alongside the Japanese, Korean and Turkish student movements. The photograph was a panoramic shot of the San Francisco city hall rotunda, city police with fire hoses and billy clubs in hand, washing dozens of students down the 36 marble steps, punishment for their attempts to be admitted to public hearings of the House Un-American Committee.

When, a month earlier, the Committee announced its impending visit and subpoenaed, among others, a Berkeley student, we immediately organized campus committees throughout the Bay Area, resurrecting the dormant structure of the ad hoc organization that we'd built a year earlier. This time, however, the congressmen missed the point and came anyway. Calling public hearings, the Committee tried to deny entrance to unfriendly onlookers, with HUAC chief investigator Wheeler serving as a one-man credentials committee. A few of us were able to get past the bouncers and prevent the hearings from proceeding by several renditions of the *Star Spangled Banner* and other Committee favorites. The first session ended at an unscheduled early hour and future sessions had a more rigorous screening to select a friendly audience. With a few thousand pickets outside, we negotiated an agreement with the Committee for seating on a first-come, first-served basis. Reaching agreement in the presence of S.F. county sheriff Matthew Carbury, who promised that law enforcement agents would absent themselves, the arrangement was almost immediately betrayed by the Committee. When students were again denied entrance to the hearing room, many sat down to sing the national anthem. Carbury kept his marshalls away, but city police moved in with hoses and clubs. Over a hundred were washed or dragged away, heads bouncing down the steps, and 64 were placed under arrest. Police casualties were placed at five; two with minor cuts, one bitten on the hand and two heart attacks. The symbolism of the heart failures was not missed by those who helped bring them on. The next day brought out 5,000 demonstrators, the largest showing in San Francisco since the labor struggles 25 years before.

The hearings themselves, presided over by Louisiana's Edwin Willis, were conducted with the expected tedium, broken occasionally by expulsions of unfriendly witnesses. Outstanding as a friendly witness was deputy customs collector Irving Fishman of the New York Port Authority, part of the regular Committee entourage. Fishman's bag (literally) was a sealed sack of alleged foreign mail, which he broke open in each town, as if for the first time, proclaiming as he spilled out its contents, "No effort is spared to flood Communist propaganda to perhaps every college, university and secondary school in the United States." Writer Milton Mayer pointed out a New York *Herald-Tribune* story about Fishman, reporting that each time he begins his routine, "the Committee members act out their part in the talking charade just as if they hadn't already seen, heard and done the same thing repeatedly." Hopefully, Chairman Willis' description of the class struggle was a one-time-only performance. "The Reds," announced the Chairman, "wish to eliminate the Bushwashee by using the Petroleum."

Sixty-three of the 64 arrested were never brought to trial, as the judge dismissed charges. A decent man though part of a dying age, the man in the black robe wasn't able to catch the drift of recent developments, describing us as "for the most part clean-cut American college students who will within the next few years enter into the business and professional worlds, and many of them, I am sure, will become leaders in their respective fields." The sixty-fourth arrestee, Bob Meisenbach, became a test case, the outcome of which was to absolve either us or the police and the Committee.

J. Edgar Hoover, appointing himself as guardian of our political virginities, issued a document *Communist Target—Youth,* warning us that we were being duped. HUAC doctored forty-five minutes of film clips, turning out a miserable little film entitled "Operation Abolition." No Leifenstahls they, the film failed in its attempt to convict Meisenbach before his trial began. Nevertheless, they circulated several hundred prints at $100 per; Standard Oil, the American Legion, Coast Federal Savings and other noted film buffs bought the flick in bulk. Our demonstrations and response to the ensuing attacks were acredited with taking most of the sting out of the Committee, an honor most likely deserved. But "Operation Abolition" at the same time was perhaps the crystalizing vehicle for the consolidation of the Birch Society and Young Americans for Freedom. Our massive campaign began with television and radio appearances, cross-country speaking tours, debates, and the distribution of hundreds of thousands of pieces of literature. Through discussions and correspondence, we sought to convince almost every significant religious group, trade union and newspaper in the country of our innocence and the Committee's guilt. And we won their support. When Meisenbach came to trial, an innocent verdict was pronounced. That was in 1960, and the Committee, with a new name, the House Internal Security Committee, and attempted new image, has ventured out of Washington only once since then.

For our efforts, and especially in response to the Meisenbach decision, a barrage of anti-Communist reactions came our way. A number of graduate students lost fellowships, grants and jobs. At least two foreign students were deported. One British student, who lived with us for a time, was featured in the newspapers the day after the mass demonstration. Wearing a raincoat and carrying an umbrella to burlesque his baptism by fire hose the day before, he announced to the press: "I lost my cherry when I was raped on the steps of city hall by San Francisco police." Within days, immigration authorities were watching our house, and our friend was followed wherever he went. One day, he walked outside and told his shadows that he was going to San Francisco and would they give him a lift since they were following him anyway. They agreed, and he brought them over to the San Francisco *Chronicle*. Walking into the newsroom with his guards behind him, he announced that he was being tailed and as a former RAF pilot, he felt it reflected poorly on the democratic tradition of Britain's closest ally. A month later, despite a front-page *Chronicle* story and editorial, he was deported to Nepal. Authorities in that Asian democracy rejected him at first because, they explained, the United States is their friend and their borders are closed to any one associated with an un-American committee.

Other anti-Communists were not as humorous. The Young People's Socialist League, and Rand Corporation intellectuals who dominated social science departments, echoed the FBI's Hoover and warned that we were not being vigilant enough in guarding our ranks against "real" subversives. *Chronicle* columnist Lucius Beebe reached an all-time zenith in incitement to violence, calling us "a nest of subversionists, pacifists and defeatist whiners . . . a sounding board for every degree of defeatism, treason and Red-petting"; "influential publicists whimpering over atomic annihilation"; "a tainted core of ideological putrescence, a whited sepulchre with treason nesting in its vitals." The university, wrote Beebe, "is as much an outpost of Russian aggression as Laos or the Congo"; and finally, "Chessman's advocates and supporters locally were recruited from one of three categories—professional exhibitionists, professional crackpots and professional subversive agitators . . . *It wasn't his crime, but his friends that made his elimination mandatory.*" (Emphasis added.)

The Berkeley movement contained a remarkable collection of extremely competent and often brilliant activists, who have since become major figures in the academy or the movement. One of the most amazing was a phenomenon known as Michael Tigar. Arriving at Berkeley on a Navy ROTC scholarship in 1958, Mike became acquainted with the movement during the Woolworth picketing. As a reporter for radio station KPFA, he covered those demonstrations and the ones that followed, including those around HUAC. The day I met him, I invited him over for dinner. Going through my bookshelf, he spotted C. Wright Mills' *The Power Elite* and asked if he could borrow it. In the middle of the night, I was awakened by his knocking on the door. He had finished the book, it was great, and did I have anything else by Mills. In response to "Operation Abolition" Mike helped make a phonograph record giving our version of the events at city hall. And he became a leading spokesman, certainly our ablest public speaker, against HUAC, debating Committee-aide Fulton Lewis III before several thousand Berkeley students and touring the state. One evening in Bakersfield, I remember being offered a police escort out of town after Mike and I debated the leaders of the local Legion post. He and I contested each other for citations by HUAC, the California State Un-American Committee, and *Tocsin*. He later became editor of the University of California *Law Review*, and, as a second-year law student, was appointed clerk to Justice Brennan of the U.S. Supreme Court. Arriving for work in Washington, Mike was told by Brennan that the job was no longer his due to his past record, an action by the Justice that *The N.Y. Times* later attributed to pressure from Honest Abe Fortas. Tigar's former classmates at law school, however, retaliated, wiring Brennan: "At least when Justice Douglas fucks someone under 25, he takes out a license."

To indicate the polluted atmosphere of the time, in 1958, California Governor Goodwin Knight was forced to run for Senator instead of his incumbent office, by then Senator William Knowland who sought the governor's mansion for himself. This prompted the *People's World* in San Francisco to headline their story with "Knight is Made a Pawn" with the subhead, "So you met someone who set you back on your heels, Goodie, Goodie." The California electorate, in a rare burst of wisdom, set both Goodie and Knowland back on their heels, and the former rose to the dubious glory of hosting a late night talk show in Los Angeles. (Knowland returned to the media also, to his family-owned Oakland *Tribune*, about which more later.)

Back in Los Angeles for the summer in 1960, I turned on the TV one night to find Goodie showing "Operation Abolition." The movie was so important, said the former governor, that he would show it again the next night. I called the studio and got permission from the Governor's secretary to appear on the show along with the film the next night. When I arrived at the studio, a group of men with clubs and bats stood guard at the parking-lot gate. The studio guard informed me that they were a safeguard "against the Reds who are expected." Coming onto the stage, I saw an audience decked out to a man in Legionaire soldier caps. The format that night called for the film being shown, followed by our discussion. While the film was on, and later, the heroic veterans attacked me with epithets of "beatnik," "pansy," "faggot," and all the rest. One guy, apparently a foot-fetishist, actually came up and, off-camera, tried to yank the shoes off my feet. A kick in his jaw produced a groan, this *on*-camera, to my embarrassment. The show over, I threw my arm around Goodie's shoulder, my other hand pumping his, all the way out to the parking lot, figuring if they get me, I'm taking the guv with me.

The next night, the film was to be shown again, and this time Knight invited four students from Berkeley and a San Francisco professor to debate HUAC investigator Wheeler and a group of Committee supporters. I picked up my friends at the airport to drive them to the studio. At the station itself, Wheeler was repeating his duties at the San Francisco hearings, telling the guards who to let into the studio and who not. The show consisted mainly of Knight calling the students names, and turning to Wheeler and friends for official substantiation. When it was over, I approached the governor and said that I thought he handled the show unfairly, that these guests had come all the way down from San Francisco to give information, and that he had behaved rudely. He turned to me and shouted, "And I think you're a bum." I responded to the effect that if he couldn't be clever, he should by all means be crude. Rising to the occasion, he swept his finger in the air and, indicating the other students, screamed, "I think you are all bums." Turning to me again: "You're Myerson, aren't you. I know you. [Anticipating me by six years:] You're a Communist, your father's a Communist, and your Grandfather's a Communist." I whispered to his face, "And how's your momma?" The legionaires moved in, and I moved out, running a gauntlet of fists, knees and hard toes.

Sitting sore and bruised later that night, I knew I had seen native fascism in action for the first time, and it was kind of chilling. I remembered that a couple of years before, some folks, testing the McCarthyist mood of the country, took the Declaration of Independence out on street-corners to try and collect signatures, going home after several hours of work, with less than a dozen names. About the time the Declaration was originally drafted, in 1776, Betsy Ross sewed the first flag to represent on cloth what Tom Jefferson said on paper. Somewhere along the line though the paper was discarded and the flag became supreme. Which is a shame. I wonder, if we ran the Delcaration of Independence up a flagpole today, how many Legionaires and police would salute it.

That summer in Los Angeles was the setting for the Democratic Convention. While news cameras were vicariously playing Peeping Tom on Jack Kennedy's boudoir in West Los Angeles, events of considerably greater significance were unfolding downtown. A mass march, under the aegis of Dr. King and A. Phillip Randolph, was organized to place demands for a civil rights plank in the party platform. Mike Harrington, one of Randolph's key operatives, had recruited me and some friends to mobilize the youth contingent. The day before the march, Linus Pauling had led several thousand of us in a peace parade through the city, also placing demands on the convention. The King-Randolph march, from the new city sports arena, the convention site, to Shrine Auditorium, featured Marion Berry and Bernard Lee, then of SNCC, who successfully lobbied in L.A. for a plank supporting the sit-ins sweeping the South.

All the candidates—Kennedy, Johnson, Symington, Stevenson, etc.—were invited to address the crowd. I was backstage when Kennedy, the last to speak, arrived. What followed was an incredible performance of mechanical man, perhaps unequaled until Stanley Kubrick gave us Hal the Computer. The moment Kennedy stepped in the stage door, an aide handed him notes for his remarks, another ran a comb through his hair, and still another whispered in his ear snatches of what earlier speakers had to say. The future President meanwhile had not broken stride as he walked from the door to the podium; he only paused a fraction of a second to throw away the notes before he reached the stage itself. The next twenty minutes were peppered with jibes at the remarks of his predecessors to the lectern.

The convention itself was more of the same. Harry Bridges had said a year before that "The fix is in for Kennedy," and nobody ever had reason to doubt the validity of Bridges' announcement. CBS captured the Big Squeeze for us millions of viewers: Richard C. Hottelet exhibiting his perpetual hysteria over inconsequentials; Howard K. Smith filling us in on parliamentary procedure, but in murmured tones, the television newscaster's equivalent of a sly wink and elbow poke in the ribs; the "personal interest" reporter embarrassing a Hollywood starlet into a foreign policy discussion; and Franklin Roosevelt, Jr., lawyer to the dictator Trujillo, being prompted by his political boss James Farley to applaud the remarks of his mother, Eleanor.

A few months later, after his election, the new President appointed his campaign manager and kid brother as Attorney General and Minister of Wiretap; the President of Ford as Secretary of Defense to replace the President of General Motors; and Dean Rusk as Secretary of State. In appointing the latter, Kennedy stated: "We hope that in the coming years the foreign policy of the United States of America will be identified in the minds of the people of the world as a policy that is not merely anti-Communist but rather for freedom." But, the London *Observer* in a point well taken, observed that we were not given an alternative to the past: "Rusk may be remembered as the Secretary of State who kept the cold war going as his predecessors have done, but more smoothly and with less vulgarity. What he may give us could be Dulles with a smile." Of course, *The Observer* can be excused for so terribly underestimating the vulgarity of the new secretary. One could not foresee with certainty the Cuban invasion, the tanks at the gates of Berlin, the missile crisis or the slaughter of the innocents in Vietnam.

But one could foresee the future direction of the Democratic and Republican Parties by observing those 1960 conventions. There is a direct line between them and 1964, with the nomination of Goldwater in San Francisco and the sabotaging of Mississippi's blacks in Atlantic City. Or from those two disasters to the police riots in Miami and Chicago in 1968. Again, Lenny Bruce: "It's so corrupt it's thrilling." But equally perceptive is Bobby Kennedy's observation of the Democratic Party: "Mayor Daley is the ball game." And will anyone ever forget that repellent little man screaming obscenities at Senator Ribicoff when the latter observed that the former's police used gestapo tactics. One imagines that Daley removed a green eyeshade from his brow only for the occasion. And has any university president, evangelist preacher or police commissioner yet upbraided the mayor for his Filthy Speech Movement?

I still feel most people, even in the movement, missed the point of Chicago. The spate of Chicago put-down lapel buttons and posters that emerged after the Democratic convention indicates that some folks think that Chicago is exceptional. But it was Berkeley where California's finest, with their long-standing rep as "good cops," promiscuously used buckshot and poison gas only eight months after Chicago. The stampede against blacks, working people and students, is hardly confined to Cook County, Illinois. I think it may have been Malcolm X who popularized the phrase Up South, to indicate the hypocrisy of the North at the height of the Southern civil rights movement. In any case, it was the concessions of the liberals and "moderates" and reformers to the racists and war-makers in Los Angeles in 1960, Atlantic City in 1964 and Chicago in 1968 that help make possible the Goldwaters and Nixons. It is the Nothern Democratic mayors Yorty, Alioto, and Daley that make Southern Justice a national phenomenon.

---

seven

*And then the President [Johnson] recited from memory
a passage from a speech he had learned for a
recitation contest at the age of 8 or 9:*

*"I have seen the glories of art and archi-
tecture, and mountain and river; I have seen
the sunset on the Jungfrau, and the full moon
rise over Mont Blanc. But the fairest vision
on which these eyes ever looked was the flag
of my country in a foreign land."*

—ASSOCIATED PRESS, 1965

*H.E.F. Donohue: Then you must think that the
    United States is an imperialistic country?
Nelson Algren: It's an imperialist son-of-a-bitch.*

—Interview with NELSON ALGREN

As chairman of SLATE, the organization that had virtual hegemony over student politics in Berkeley, I had formed a close working relationship with the people in the American Friends Service Committee, the Quaker action group that led the Bay Area ban-the-bomb and antishelter movements. Upon graduation in 1961, I was offered the job as AFSC Peace Secretary in San Francisco, but the offer was quickly withdrawn because, I learned later, of anti-Communist pressure from "friends" in the Socialist Party and Americans for Democratic Action. (A subsequent job offer of a similar nature with the AFSC in New York was likewise voided.)

Dick Rettig, president of the National Student Association and a house guest when in Berkeley, asked us to come to the NSA convention in Madison, Wisconsin, to help lead the liberal caucus and fight through a strong anti-HUAC resolution. A couple of us had decided to leave Berkeley anyway. Even in high school I felt more embarrassment than resentment for graduating hangers-on. I've never been very comfortable in school and usually despised it thoroughly. Once I left a school, I was not about to return, and I had much difficulty in empathizing with those who could. Once free of the University of California, I wanted to move as far away as possible. New York it was to be. Where else?

We stopped over in Madison on the way, and renewed acquaintances with Tom Hayden and Al Haber who, representing the embryonic Students for a Democratic Society, were heading up the liberal caucus. Cocky as we were, we figured to imbue the caucus with a little Berkeley pizzazz for a day or so, and then say goodbye to the student movement forever. And that is what we did.

Four days later, I was in New York looking for a job. Politics in the big city was something else again. However fragile the unity of the Bay Area movement, there was at least a semblance of togetherness. New York's Left resembled the classic juvenile gang situation, with nobody crossing over to another's turf without expecting to get his ass kicked around the block. That winter, I remember, Young Americans for Freedom, backed by a collection of equally enlightened co-sponsors, called a mass meeting in Madison Square Garden, inviting Barry Goldwater, Strom Thurmond and other imperial wizards to display their intellectual wares. Featured speaker was to be Moshe Tshombe, then doing the bidding of Union Haute Miniere in the Congo.

Well, thought I, what better situation around which to pull folks together in New York. If people could not agree on what they were for, there should at least be unanimity about what they were against. Being a neutral, read unknown, force as a foreigner in the city, I was able to call together perhaps 30 representatives of organizations which hadn't spoken with one another in years: civil liberties unions, socialist sects, youth organizations, a number of black groups, various peace committees. Having drawn together my mini-ecumenical council, I decided to get out while the getting was good. After original minimal agreement on demonstration tactics at the Garden rally, the group began to splinter. The night of the action, newsmen, displaying their perennial ignorance of the Left, found a common face to the demonstration. This was personally gratifying, of course. But in fact only the time and place were commonly agreed to, and the picket line was actually three different lines with separate leaderships and slogans, and they ringed the Garden in sections. Most of the sins and few of the virtues of American radicalism were present at that, my debut in New York.

SANE, the major force in the New York peace movement, had responded to Senator Dodd's Internal Security Subcomittee by holding hearings of its own to purge itself of what Robert Welch likes to call "comsymps." I recalled Mort Sahl's line: "Every time the Russians arrest an American, the United States retaliates and arrests an American." One especially distressing sign of the times was the front page photo on *The Times* of Jack Kennedy at a White House party, flanked on one arm by SANE chairman Norman Cousins, on the other by General Maxwell Taylor.

SDS was then the youth affiliate of the anti-Communist League for Industrial Democracy, a liberal research organization with establishment, ex-socialist, labor spokesmen such as Victor Reuther and David Dubinsky as sponsors. While SDS was programmatically independent of its elder patrons, it was finanically very much dependent. With the dissolution of Student SANE by the parent group which saw its offspring turning Red, SDS began to fill a vacuum in student peace activity. Together with the Student Peace Union, then the youth group favored by anti-Communist liberals because of its YPSL leadership, the SDS organized the February 1962 peace march on Washington. Permeating the march's statement of purpose was the position of opposition to the Soviet Union, suggesting that the way to fight "them" is with such measures as the Alliance for Progress rather than the arms races. The arms race was opposed because it was an ineffective as well as dangerous method of dealing with "the real Soviet danger." The President, knowing where the smart money was, served coffee and donuts on the White House lawn to the young protesters.

Commented *Sanity* magazine, now defunct, then issued in Madison by former Student SANE leaders: "What is lacking among the students is comprehension of the arms race in terms of the cold war: Any questions which would expose the complex relationship between, say, the armaments industry and the cold war, are evaded. . . . [Most students' understanding] of the cold war is that it is caused by Soviet 'expansionism' which is opposed primarily militarily by the United States, and that the solution lies mainly in disarmament, which can be brought about by unilateral initiatives to relieve tension. That the United States has a significant stake in the cold war, both militarily and economically, that the Soviet Union might be economically favored by disarmament —that, indeed, the plans for disarmament with inspections, and disengagement in Central Europe, which the students advanced have been proposed by the Soviet bloc—are among issues which the students do not face."

Student SANE was of course dismissed as Red. As was I, when I accepted the task, at a University of Chicago conference, of organizing and heading up the U.S. contingent to the World Youth Festival, being held the next summer in Helsinki. That was the year that mass suicide was popularized with the near-satirical slogan, "Better Dead Than Red." Only matched by the criminal insanity fostered by white people's attitudes towards blacks was the anti-Communist hysteria. Alongside each bomb shelter was tacked the new Golden Rule: Kill thy neighbor before he killeths thou. Red equalled bad, and should Communists favor the Salk vaccine, we had no choice but to promote polio.

Senator Barry Goldwater, in his monumental work, *Conscience of a Conservative*, which might have been ghost-written by James Thurber in his more comic moments, made the point that the Moyseyev Dancers should never be allowed to perform in this country because they tended to ease cold-war tensions inasmuch as the dancers gave the impression that some Russians were nearly human. North American know-nothingism reached new highs that autumn when Richard Nixon, fighting the Hollywood Hills fire to save his $125,000 home, complained that he had seen many tragedies and horrible conditions throughout the world, but nothing so bad as the flame approaching his house from a half-mile away.

President Kennedy's envoys were then negotiating with the Cuban government to exchange farm machinery for the CIA Cubans captured at Playa Giron, a trade that the media here felt inhuman, but which we captioned, "Tractors for Traitors, or Caterpillars for Worms." The mentality that produced the Playa

Giron invasion prevailed; the Supreme Court ruled that all suspected Communists had to register to the essential effect that they were spies. In Texas, it was a capital crime to be a Communist. The Florida State Supreme Court ruled in a case dealing with the NAACP that anyone accused of being a Red is automatically suspect and therefore not accorded the same rights as others. The highest court in the land had already ruled, in a California union-management dispute, that contracts with suspected Communists needn't be abided by. And that fall, news fillers reported that one of the relocation camps, to be used to round up all suspected future subversives should a national emergency be declared, had just been repainted.

Nelson Algren tells a story about his getting ready to leave a party and reaching the door, only to be insulted by one of the hosts and being told he should take off; at which point he plops into the nearest chair as if to say he was just then getting comfortable. That approximated my mood in those days. With such rampant anti-Communism in the air, I decided, "fuck it, I'm staying." So I took the job with the festival committee working with, among others, some Communists. Invariably the first question I was asked by friends in the National Student Association was where the committee got its money, as if this would reveal its hidden sinister qualities. They were of course disappointed to learn that its money came, naturally enough, from the participants' fees and various fund appeals and that sinister qualities must be searched for elsewhere. That NSA, it turns out, was on the take from the CIA did not matter. It accepted the cold war, siding with the angels.

A curious elitism had developed. Friends of deep conscience were unable to accept that millions of people are willingly, consciously committed to Marxism, and with the same deep humanism that they nurtured. Whatever opposition these friends felt to U.S. Government policies, was limited to that: some policies were aberrations of a system in fact more truly perfect than any other. We cannot accept Cuba, they would say, because Castro had not been elected; we cannot accept Guinea because it jails counter revolutionaries; Algeria uses violent resistance in its national struggle, India removed the Portuguese from Goa by force, Japan marched in the streets to prevent our President's visit. We don't understand that some countries believe there is no political freedom without economic freedom, that voting at age 21 doesn't matter if your life expectancy is 28. We cannot accept mass demonstrations and marching and violence; people should go to the ballot box; the vote every four years for picked candidates is real democracy. We advocate an updated version of the white man's burden but we won't call it that.

They continue: we must sometimes become undemocratic to maintain our democracy. We must maintain control of the organizations in which we work, and exclude those who may be friendly to the devil. For he is a conspirator, highly organized, and able to wield influence over masses of people. Therefore we cannot allow masses of people to come together except as we organize them. And we must exclude the conspirator, even if he agrees with us, even if he accepts our leadership, because he is not to be trusted. And if he is elected, we must remove him from office for the sake of democracy. And though we thus become ineffective and unable to build a mass movement in this country, it is a minor loss for we basically and fundamentally accept the assumptions of the government whose policies we oppose. Besides we have been taught by our professors, members of Americans for Democratic Action, that masses are always undemocratic if allowed to control governments or organizations. A plague on all houses except our own.

A major objection against my working for the festival committee was that the main organizational support of the festival itself came from the World Federation of Democratic Youth (WFDY). Organized in London in 1945, WFDY was formed by representatives of youth organizations, Communist and non-Communist, from all continents. U.S. delegates represented the NAACP, the YMCA, a number of radical youth groups, etc. Offices were set up in Paris, but the cold war forced the federation to move to Budapest, where it still resides. WFDY's U.S. affiliates dropped out, but with the coming of political independence in Africa, Asia and Latin America, new member organizations, representing millions, joined. Even today, WFDY represents perhaps a quarter-billion youths, but none in the United States. A student counterpart to WFDY, the International Union of Students with headquarters in Prague, representing the overwhelming majority of the world's students, also played a major role in the organization of the festival. That year, 1962, while NSA and the international confederation to which it is affiliated (also a CIA recipient) were admonishing me not to help organize the festival because it would be unrepresentative, they refused to recognize as legitimate the pro-independence university federation of Puerto Rico, causing the departure of a dozen other federated student unions.

In 1962, the student movement in this country was most provincial. The United States is traditionally a nation woefully ignorant of the rest of the world. Since the 19th century and the drive West, when it was our manifest destiny to slaughter the Indian population and annex half of Mexico, our country has suffered from "big-nation chauvinism." How many of even the most thoughtful of us know anything about Vietnam, even today after that nation has occupied this country's mind for seven full years. Never before in our history has there been a poetry boom as there is today, but how many here know any Vietnamese poets, though poetry is a national pastime in Vietnam. Of course, since 1962 the Cuban revolution and the Vietnam war have had major impact on young North Americans. Both movements have in large part consisted of young people, both are led by Communists, both are poor and colored, both have brought down upon themselves the wrath of the most militarily powerful country in the history of the world. But both continue to win, both have been battlegrounds over which the United States brought the world to the brink of thermonuclear incineration, and both have increasingly won the respect and admiration of large numbers of American youth. Older radicals often have difficulty understanding that Cuba and Vietnam are to younger people today what the Soviet Union was for them. And for the same reasons. What the defense of the Soviet Union meant two decades ago, the defense of Cuba and Vietnam has meant in the sixties. The latter two revolutions are "ours" as the Soviet "belonged" to earlier generations. At the same time, people new to the movement today, retaining anti Communist biases with which they were raised, are severely mistaken in separating Cuba and Vietnam from a process that began in October, 1917, in Petrograd. Their estimate of the Soviet Union is immensely different from that of their contemporaries in Cuba and Vietnam.

Since 1962, young people have become more internationally conscious. Young blacks in growing numbers came to feel an affinity for their African brothers. SNCC leaders made tours of African revolutionary capitals and when Julian Bond was denied his seat in the Georgia legislature, some dozen or so African delegations paid him tribute at the United Nations. His own country's UN delegation, shamefully, did not. A spate of visits to Vietnam and Cuba have brought much closer to home the meaning of those two revolutions, and the May 1968 events in France destroyed for more advanced political young people here whatever illusions they harbored of the co-optation of workers in a capitalist society. Much ignorance remains of course. In late 1966, Luis Turcios died at the age of 24. One of the great heroes of our generation, Turcios remains unknown to most of his contemporaries and even to those here who would consider themselves his compatriots. But in his native Guatemala and its sister Latin American states, Luis Turcios Lima was known as the head of the Rebel Armed Forces.

Buried less than 24 hours after his body was found, his funeral, according to *The Times,* was attended by 1,500 people in a driving tropical storm—this in a country under the domination of Green Berets, the CIA and United Fruit Company, where torture and death are common for opponents of the regime. Yet it is perhaps an overestimation to say five percent of today's SDS membership knows of Turcios.

In 1962, however, few movement people even really knew of Guatemala. And that is when I was trying to recruit several hundred to go to Helsinki to meet with their opposite numbers from other lands. The job was not without its pleasures. I remember traveling to Washington once every couple of weeks to arrange post-festival tours of various countries. The Soviet embassy in Washington is around the corner from the American Legion national headquarters, and one day, coming out of the embassy with piles of Soviet propaganda and literature in one attaché case, I found I had a half-hour to blow before my next appointment. Out of curiosity I meandered over to the Legion building. Met by an armed guard, I identified myself as a member of NYU Young Americans for Freedom, and was ushered up to their Americanism department. There I filled up another case, with HUAC reports, Hoover declarations and other Legion material. Like a schizophrenic Willie Loman, I wandered around Washington that day, Communist literature in one hand, anti-Communist in the other. There was no doubt where I was at: on the train coming home I found in the Legion's bulletin *Firing Line* two references to myself as a Communist agent.

A carnival of ludicrousness was performed in the media over the festival. *Reader's Digest,* with the largest readership in the nation, asked in the title of its piece, "Is Finland Playing Russian Roulette?" Victor Riesel turned over his syndicated column to the FBI's Hoover. With his unusual gift for imprecision, Riesel introduced the column: "In this columning business, you get to know many public personalities. Some are always understanding of their need to use their influence and positions for the greatest common welfare. I have found my good friend J. Edgar Hoover a man of all these qualities. In addition, in his field, he is the greatest scientist of all." The "scientist" himself went on to expound on how "the Communist movement is currently concentrating great effort in the youth field." *Newsweek* warned of how Helsinki, "the White City of the North" would become "tinted an embarrassing shade of pink."

The Central Intelligence Agency, in all its infinite wisdom, had set up, in 1959, just before the previous festival in Vienna, an operation called the Independent Research Service. At that time it was directed by Harvard professor Paul Sigmund, now on the Princeton faculty. But for the Helsinki festival, IRS leadership fell to *New York* magazine writer Gloria Steinem and Dennis Shaul. Dennis, who had been student government president at Notre Dame was rewarded for his CIA apprenticeship at IRS by being chosen NSA president the following year. With an $80,000 budget, IRS officers toured the country holding indoctrination briefings, and propagandizing college students in order to recruit "good" participation at Helsinki. (Our committee's policy in organizing the contingent was first come, first served, so there were no political barriers to those who came under IRS auspices.) IRS recruitees held sessions on how to answer embarassing questions in Europe about racism, U.S. support for fascist regimes, etc. Eventually, of the 450-member U.S. contingent in Helsinki, maybe 60 or 70 were IRS apologists, and most of these were recruited out of SDS, Student Peace Union, AFSC and other liberal groupings. I spent much of my time during that year of festival preparation touring the country, retracing earlier paths traveled in the anti-HUAC campaign. Frequently Dennis and I would find ourselves in the same place, and debates were then arranged. When in New York, Dennis or Gloria would call me to have lunch, each of us carrying out one-man search-and-destroy missions.

One day I received a call from a Walter Kirschenbaum, who identified himself as a producer of the Barry Gray show, New York's most popular late-night radio talk show. Kirschenbaum, whom I learned wrote for CIA-recipient *New Leader* magazine under the name "Walter K. Lewis," wanted to arrange for Gloria and me to appear on the Gray program. Just before we went on the air Barry Gray, looking like the little man on top of the wedding cake, leaned over and asked Gloria for a date after the show, giving me some indication that I would not be favored with generosity in the questioning that was to follow. In fact, every question in the first fifteen minutes was directed at me. None dealt with the festival, the subject about which I was presumably invited to speak. Barry, with immaculate disdain, would grin and ask, for example: "When I say 'Communism' what do you think of first." Playing his word-association game, I would grin back and mumble, "One-third of the world." On and on it went. Pretty soon, Kirschenbaum or K. Lewis or whatever the masked man was really called began bringing questions up to Barry to ask me, these dealing with such germane subjects as did-I-know-so-and-so or was-I-at-such-and-such-a-meeting-the-night-of-etc. Obviously I'd walked into a set-up. I had seen my duty and I had done it and rose to leave. Gray immediately started to shift the questions, of a different order, to Gloria. When the show finally ended and the red light went off, signaling we were off the air, a page boy came in to announce, "Phone call for Mr. Kirschenbaum from Mr. Rommerstein." Herbert Rommerstein, New York FBI agent, was calling to offer congratulations for a job well done.

The next morning, arriving at my office, I found a telegram from James Wechsler, New York *Post* editor, saying he'd heard the program and would I call him. He asked me down to his office. When I walked in, he pulled out a bottle, poured drinks, and began to tell me he'd been fascinated by the Gray show, that he "too" had once been a real comer in "the Communist youth movement" and how did I come to be where I was at. After about two hours of drinking and fending him off, I left. Next day's Wechsler column began, "By some simple standards, Michael Myerson is a dangerous character," and built from there. Shit, I thought, sometimes I feel I'm becoming paranoid, but I really *know* I'm being persecuted.

The World Youth Festival for Peace and Friendship was an omnibus affair, ten days of concerts and performances (the Bolshoi, Ballet Africaine, etc.), sports events with champion athletes, interdelegation meetings, scientific discussions and political forums. Its obvious assets were at the same time its main drawbacks. With 15,000 participants from 130 countries, supported by the All-China Youth Federation and UNESCO affiliates, Ho Chi Minh and William Tubman, it did promote "peace and friendship." But the immensity of the operation and the variance of participants made difficult discussions of depth and substance. Conferences are always a drag for me, the only antidote being the fine art of coffee-klatching.

I was in Helsinki several weeks before the festival to help finalize accommodations and arrangements for the Yanks. My Canadian and Cuban counterparts were immediately friendly, but most of the delegation leaders harbored suspicions, in large part due to the CIA operations at the Vienna Festival. Their skepticism was more than a little valid: the Korean, for example, had been buried alive by a U.S. tank during the war in his country.

When people later asked what the festival was like, I could never answer; I did not see it. With only a half-dozen snatches of sleep, I played scout-master to hundreds of young Americans, answering complaint after complaint (The water is too hot; the water is too cold, etc.). At the one event that I attended, a concert featuring Archie Shepp, I took several offerings from Yevtushenko's vodka flask and blissfully passed out. Marilyn Monroe had died that morning and I really wasn't up to fielding everybody's bitch. I had always had a deep sympathy for Marilyn. A perfect example of midcentury Americana, she was the self as consumer product. Abused and used by others all her life, she had finally called an end to it all. And hanging my mental flag at half-mast, I held a one-man work stoppage for the rest of the day.

Meanwhile, back home at the wrench, U.S. newspapers were reporting large scale riots by Finnish youth in protest against the festival. In fact, a few dozen Finnish kids had started throwing rocks at African delegates, shouting racist epithets. Simultaneously, a Brazilian and Cuban conga line, snake-dancing down Helsinki's main drag, was attacked. Fighting broke out, and there were recurrences over the next 24 hours. At one point, Cuban exiles, who had somehow found their way up to Finland that week, attacked some Cuban festival participants. Accusations of CIA involvement were disregarded by United Press International. By the time the fracas was over, perhaps 3,000 persons had been involved. Prime Minister Kekkonen came to attend festival events in protest of the street harassment. Flooded with telegrams from worried parents back in the states, we called a press conference to announce that no U.S. participants were hurt. More press attention was given though to a fight between myself and Charles Wiley. An HUAC informer attending as the representative of a New York radio station when he returned to the States, he was chief witness for HUAC in its hearings on the Vienna festival. That committee seems to have set a cut-off point on the intelligence quotients of its friendly witnesses, confining its standards to the 60's and 70's. Some testified that people were in both Helsinki and San Francisco simultaneously, others talked about a "Finnish Fish Festival." The California state senate hearings were a bit more accurate if only because they seem somehow to have acquired the one list of U.S. participants missing from our office, and reprinted it in its entirety.

On the way up to Helsinki, we had stopped in at the Brussels' festival office. A friend working there invited us up to Antwerp that night, where a visiting Czech cultural troupe was giving a benefit performance for the Belgian delegates to Helsinki. After the show, we were invited to a left youth club, where everyone was dancing the twist to Ray Charles records. A young boy came up and asked if we had a place to stay, insisting on taking us home with him. On the outskirts of Antwerp we entered a little thatched-roofed house. The walls were lined with African masks and other objects and when I inquired about it, he told me Patrice Lumumba used to stay with his family when he was in Belgium. The next morning, exchanging addresses, I asked where I could write him. He toed the ground in embarrassment and said that it would be best for me, being an American, not to write him: "My father is general secretary of the Communist Party here." This was 24 hours after landing in Europe, My First Trip to Europe, that uniquely North American college graduate experience, the last in a succession of Firsts: First Date, First Trip to Grand Canyon, First Shave.

Six months in Europe followed—in Scandinavia, Eastern Europe, Italy, and England. I came home with three firm conclusions: North Americans are the most politically ignorant of peoples; the least class-conscious; and the least aware of the ravages of war. All of these were of course revelations to no one but myself, but they had a strong impact on my still impressionable mind. I was in Budapest for about a month, working for WFDY, in late 1962. Returning to my hotel one night, I received a call from a Canadian friend at WFDY asking me to come to his place right away, U.S. ships were blockading Cuba where missiles had been discovered, and Soviet ships were on their way. All night long a group of us, North Americans, Cubans, and Arabs stayed up listening to Radio Budapest, Radio Moscow and Voice of America trying to make sense of the October Missile Crisis. I said, goddamnit, let's march on the U.S. legation in Budapest. The Hungarian brothers cautioned me against that, apparently because of some tender diplomatic problems having to do with Cardinal Mindzenty's tenancy in the building, a difficulty I was not adverse to disregarding given the seriousness of the present crisis. The next day saw the first demonstration, this against the Americans of course, of Hungarian students since 1956. I was so damned frustrated. I knew I couldn't explain, in those circumstances, what the U.S. was all about to inquiring Hungarians. So I passed myself off as Canadian, and asked to leave Hungary. On behalf of the WFDY secretariat, I drew up an appeal to U.S. youth organizations. Together with thousands of letters to youth groups around the world, I drove the 50 kilometers to Vienna where Western mail services would guarantee faster delivery of the various messages I carried.

Checking for mail at American Express in Vienna I was astonished. A number of messages were waiting for me. One, from a friend in New York, suggested I head for Switzerland and watch the missiles pass overhead. Another, from a relative who worked for Sears, told of a run on guns in fear of a Cuban invasion. In Los Angeles! Four or five told of friends, packing their few belongings and trunksful of canned goods, and heading for the mountains. Most discouraging was the report that a good friend on the Fair Play for Cuba Committee (and today a frequent visitor to Cuba) accused Fidel, at a San Francisco rally, of selling out the revolution by accepting missiles in the first place.

By the time I had reached Vienna, the crisis fortunately passed. Then the more gruesome facts became apparent. *Look* reported that, moments before the Soviet ships pulled back, word had been given that nuclear weapons were to be used if necessary; and that the Cabinet, most Supreme Court justices, other high government officials and their families were on their way to their secret bomb shelters in Virginia. Now, that's pretty fucking terrifying. They were prepared to do us all in. And that was Jack Kennedy, our "most progressive" President in 25 years. The illusions people carry, even today, of their exemption from the crimes of the U.S. government never fail to amaze me. Perhaps the most incredible and bizarre aspect of being part of the wealthiest nation in history, and the most criminal, is the absolute alienation that exists between citizen and government action. That folks can sit down to a meal of fried chicken while watching the Huntley-Brinkley show may be pretty weird. But perhaps the atrocity photos we have been subjected to now for half a dozen years were designed to make us accept our role as the New Nazis.

The Dallas *Morning News* of January 1, 1963, quoted an account of our pacification program in Vietnam: "In the province of Kien-Tuong, seven villagers were led to the town square. Their stomachs were slashed, their livers extracted and put on display. These victims were women and children. In another village, a dozen mothers were decapitated before the eyes of compatriots. In still another village, expectant mothers were invited to the square by Government forces to be honored. Their stomachs were ripped and unborn babies removed." *Life* magazine, that same week, displayed a photo of two U.S. Marines smiling down on dead Vietnamese peasants, a scene reminiscent of captured Nazi photos. Other pictures show napalmed peasant huts. The San Francisco *Chronicle* that November 9, ran an AP report of one village: "Scores of students of both sexes declared that military and police inquisitors forced them to drink soapy water until their intestines poured blood. . . . One young girl, found praying with a crowd at Saigon's Xa Loi Buddhist pagoda, said electrodes from the generator of a field radio were attached to her breasts while she was in custody." A year later, on September 17, 1964, an AP photo caption in the *Herald-Tribune* read, "A Vietnamese marine follows a captive Viet Cong suspect as they carry the heads of a Viet Cong platoon leader and two soldiers on a pole between them after a battle near Can Duoc, 30 miles south of Saigon, Sept. 16. The battle was between battalion-sized forces. Heads, cut from men killed in engagement, were suspended by the ears to be carried off as trophies."

Those accounts were, once again, written in 1963 and 1964, and still the war is with us; still folks sit down to dinner to hear the roll call of death; still they feel no connection with the action of their government; still there is no gut-reaction to the fact that the reported 100 or 200 dead reported today are dead in their name; let alone the 25 or 30 dead in Detroit last week, or Oakland next month. Even today, June 22, 1969, as I write these words, *The New York Times* Sunday travel section carries a letter to the editor: "To anyone who is hesitating about going to Haiti, my advice is: *Don't hesitate—go!* My wife and I had the pleasure of visiting this beautiful island a short time ago and we were positively charmed with it. The people are very nice, the hotels are all that could be desired, the prices are reasonable and the scenery is breathtaking." It is not as though the writer knows that the Haitian per capita income hovers around $50, that the repression by the regime is perhaps the very worst in the world, that life expectancy is the lowest in the hemisphere, that an armed struggle against the government is beginning to develop. In fact, having spent time there, the tourist still doesn't know a fucking thing about Haiti away from his luxury hotel. There is no real connection between the lives of Haitians and his own, and if he did understand that there was a connection, there's a betting chance he still wouldn't care. It's enough to give you an Excedrin headache.

eight

"*You're a Sap, Mr. Jap.*"
"*We're Going to Find the Fellow Who is Yellow and Beat Him Red, White and Blue.*"
"*We've Got to Do a Job on the Japs, Baby.*"
"*They're Going to Be Playing Taps on the Japs.*"
"*The Japs Haven't Got a Chinaman's Chance.*"
"*Goodbye Mama, I'm Off to Yokahama.*"
"*Slap the Jap Right Off the Map.*"
"*To Be Specific, It's Our Pacific.*"
"*When Those Little Yellow Bellies Meet the Cohens and the Kelleys.*"

—Popular song titles during World War II

"*When your precious underprivileged get together—Oh, boy!*"
—*Dialogue from* Citizen Kane

Back from the European sojourn, I was offered a job with the California State Department of Public Health. Actually I was being hired as assistant to the director of the state poverty program, but funds were not to be available for a few months, and the public health job would serve to tide me over. Shortly after the job began, I received greetings from my draft board, inviting me down for a free physical examination and promising to reward me with induction should I prove fit.

Now, I'd always had a peculiar mental block against the possibility of being drafted. Most of my friends worried to the point of depression at the thought of serving the nation in uniform. They went to great lengths to avoid it, most of which by now are well known—playing gay, cutting off a finger, contracting diseases, shooting up dope. One swallowed a pint of blood before entering the induction center, then vomited it all up once inside. I never was concerned though. I didn't know how yet, but I never had a doubt that I wasn't going into this man's Army. Passing the physical without problems (so careful was the inspection, a Quasimodo or Rumpelstiltskin would easily slip by), we were taken into another room. There were perhaps 30 of us wondering what the next hurdle was to be, when two soldiers strode into the room. One began passing out a legal-size form to each of us. It contained the names of some 400 groups and organizations, and we had to "X" under yes or no whether we did now or had ever belonged to, known someone who did, gave money, attended a function of, subscribed to a publication of, any of the above. Most of the listed groups were defunct long before our births, and the thought occurred to me that claiming membership in one of these might de facto make me physically exempt from the draft.

The other soldier began to read, à la Jack Webb, our instructions: "The-paper-you-are-about-to-sign-may-be-the-most-important-one-you-will-sign-the-rest-of-your-lives-because-the-uniform-of-the-United-States-soldier-represents-honor-and-dignity-through-out-the-world. [Pause for effect.] Now-the-only-grounds-on-which-you-can-refuse-to-sign-is-the-Fifth-Amendment-to-the-Constitution-which-says-that-you-don't-have-to-sign-if-you-think-you're-guilty. [Another pause; then as an afterthought:] And-no-loyal-American-need-fear-signing." Now, I've never laid claims to being another William Douglas exactly, but it seemed to me the sergeant's interpretation of the Highest Law in the Land fell a bit short of what the founding fathers had in mind back there in the city of brotherly love's Independence Hall in 1787. I started to write on the form in the space reserved for elaboration: "I re——" at which point one soldier, peering over my shoulder, barked: "Not down there" (and moving my pen up to the yes column) "Up here." "No," I balked, "down here." And continued: "——fuse to sign on the grounds of the First and Fifth Amendments." The one soldier called his partner over, who in turn opened the door and called for an MP. "Stand up, wise guy, and come with me."

What followed was an hour and a half of questioning in television police style, one guy the nice and understanding big brother, the other a gorilla lurking in the back, threatening to intervene should the first guy fail. Seeking, I suppose, to learn if I was a pacifist, they asked if an ape were raping my mother would I come to her aid. I wondered aloud what his thought process had been in developing that particular question. After my broken record of "I-refuse-to-answer" I was sent home with the assurance that "You'll be hearing from us." In fact, I "heard" from them a week later, when they showed up on my job for further questioning. End of job. Three more jobs passed by the boards in quick succession as I continued to "hear" from the U.S. Army.

It seems a little on the bizarre side, but then these are grotesque times. Only a few years before, HUAC heard testimony to the effect that one way to tell a Red is by the language he uses, words like "militant" and "hootenanny" being dead giveaways.

Now there was a network television show called "Hootenanny" and Hal Zeigler, who had previously achieved fame as the producer of "Chanukah at Santa Monica" and "Borsht-Capades," both with Mickey Katz, was sponsoring a road show of unknown folk-singers, called "Hootenanny '63," and packing them into the rafters. "That's the new word, kid, hoot," explained Zeigler, "it means loot."

Elsewhere in the world of Show Biz, the equal of which there is no biz, other historic breakthroughs were being made. Sheila Graham reported that Seven Arts president Ray Stark told her: "When I tried to register 'The Bitch' as a title with the Motion Pictures Producers Association, they informed me that it couldn't be done. 'But it's the story of Lassie's mother,' " he told them. Which of course it wasn't. "Then," Ray said, "I tried to register 'Love Is a Four Letter Word.' and they said no, that wasn't permissible because of the connotation. Okay, then 'Love Is Not a Four Letter Word.' " The answer was still no. "How about 'Love Is a Five Letter Word?' " Ray requested. That was fine but it was pointed out to him that the word love has only four letters. His final title: "Love Is Not a Five Letter Word."

Along similar lines was Dr. Max Rafferty, California State Superintendent of Public Instruction, asking to ban from the schools *A Dictionary of American Slang* because, "There are words and phrases in this book I never heard of," which is the equivalent of burning all abstract art as pornography. Not since Otto Preminger went on a search for a Saint Joan and discovered Jean Seberg in a popularity contest had there been such an ill-suited People's Choice. Until Dr. Max came along and branded the afore-mentioned *Dictionary* a "practicing handbook of sexual perversion." Like galloping crud, the anti-porn fever spread. The Women's Protective League hired Richard Cotten to report that "Red agents in the U.S. are using it in devious plots and Russians in Russia are using this slang dictionary to show Americans are decadent." Cotten, his speech interrupted repeatedly by heavy applause, described himself as "a born-again Christian, an old alcoholic, a repentant sinner and an old Navy man" who had recently quit his salesman's job to become "a full-time conservative." In going his mentor, Rafferty, one better he had become, as the French say, more Catholic than the Pope. Cotten had gathered together seven pages of excerpts of the dictionary's dirty words. "I hope you will distribute them at PTA meetings," he said, "we want to flood the state with them." In response to one state assemblyman's criticism that by circulating the excerpts, he would be appealing to teen-agers' prurient interests, Cotton said, "I don't care if every teenager in California reads the filthy excerpts we're showing. What we're aiming to do is protect unborn generations." Meanwhile, copies of the controversial dictionary were discovered on the shelves of the California State Library in Sacramento, a branch of Dr. Rafferty's department. Asked why he had not removed them from the shelves, Rafferty replied: "I'm not in the business of throwing my weight around."

In one of the more curious displays of the unity of church and state, the U.S. Post Office Department canceling machines printed over stamps the words, "Pray for Peace." The irony was heightened when that same month saw the first self-immolations of Vietnamese Buddhists. Another peak was reached in modernizing Roman Catholic mores when United, TWA and American airlines reported that "The Vatican has granted a special dispensation from the laws of abstinence for Catholics traveling on United [or TWA or American] Airlines. On Fridays and all other days of abstinence you may eat the meat served during your United flight." Thus balm was offered to air passengers of all beliefs and nonbeliefs, no longer forced to consume reconstituted baked halibut.

1963 was a year, as Walter Cronkite used to say, filled with those events that alter and illuminate our times. Associated Press reported from Houston that "Mrs. Cecil Blaffer Hudson, winner of $6.5 million in a divorce action, said yesterday she had achieved an ambition—she received a larger settlement than Bobo Rockefeller's $5.5 million. . . . Brunette Mrs. Hudson, 43, mother of two sons and a patron of the arts, sighed: 'At last it's over. I'm so happy I could sing.' " And in Southampton, Long Island, only spitting distance from the digs of Jay Gatsby, a dance for 750 guests was given in honor of the coming out of debutante Fernanda Wanamaker Wetherill. The decor, reported *The Times,* "was predominantly in shades of pink and reminiscent of a garden at Versailles. . . . Three pink marquees (one for cocktails and two for supper) were pitched on the lawn to the rear of the house and the large dance marquee, also pink, on the west side of the house. Here a fountain with a gazebo over it played in the center of the dance floor, which was set up in the sunken rose garden. The orchestra was seated on the terrace at the far end of the pavilion. Urns and statues with arrangements and headdresses of flowers flanked the perimeter of the marquee and the shrubbery was alive with pink and white bee lights." *The Times* reporter unfortunately left early, but Associated Press went the distance. When the ball was over, the real party began. Reports AP: "127 socialites, age 18 to 22, went on a rampage in a nearby oceanfront mansion that had been rented as a guest house. Chief Donald J. Finlay of the village police said damage estimates ranged up to $10,000. Hundreds of windows were broken. Furniture was smashed. An expensive chandelier was torn from the ceiling. The debutante's ball broke up at 7 A.M. Sunday. At 4 P.M. that day police rounded up 30 young men who were still at the house. No charges were placed." Miss Wetherill's party took place three days after the March on Washington for Jobs and Freedom, for which the city fathers sent folks home from work and closed the liquor stores, presumably to prevent any disturbances of private property.

Other private property was disposed when the nation's seven original astronauts sold their interest in a luxury motel near Cape Kennedy, nearly doubling their money. Together with their non-salaried lawyer, the astronauts had invested more than $100,000 in the $1.6 million Cape Colony Inn and convention hall in Cocoa Beach. Apparently more incentives than God and country help our modern Christopher Columbuses in their search for distant planets. Meanwhile in the nation's capital, the late Drew Pearson reported that Senator John Stennis, against whom have been made no removal procedures à la Adam Powell, was being less than frugal with the national treasury. Stennis, from the country's poorest state, Mississippi, had the U.S. Air Force send two airplanes to carry himself and Arkansas Senator John McClellan home from Spain; the estimated cost was $20,000. Expense vouchers for the junket showed that the two Senators spent a whopping $37,810.11 for hotels, night clubs, excursions, souvenirs, etc., reported Pearson. An attaché of the U.S. embassy in Rome said, "I paid all expenses up to date, including rental of vehicles, whiskey, Kleenex, etc." The syndicated columnist inferred that the Air Force may have been motivated to fly two empty planes across the Atlantic because it needed the two votes back home to bless a big contract with AT & T.

The administrative branch of our checks-and-balances trinity was not to be outdone by the legislative wing. Deputy Defense Secretary Roswell Gilpatric's law firm became counsel for General Dynamics one month after the corporation was awarded the seven billion dollar TFX airplane contract. Gilpatric pleaded, in answer to suggestions that he step aside in Pentagon dealings with any of his previous clients, that he would be eliminated from so many decisions that he could not serve effectively.

Air Force officer and U.S. Senator Barry Goldwater, opening up his campaign for the Republican presidential nomination, declared: "I don't object to dictatorships as violently as some people do, because I realize that not all people in this world are ready for democratic processes." And echoing Goldwater's bravado was the nation's largest newspaper, *The Daily News* of New York. In its daily editorial decision for Christ, *The News,* commenting on the murder by three N.Y. detectives of a homicide suspect, while he slept in his hotel room, declared: "The men who saved the taxpayers the expense of trying Falco for murder were Det. Lt. Thomas Quinn, Capt. C.T.J. Meyer, and Det. Cornelius Carroll— all of whom we're delighted to congratulate on a job well done. . . . What we like about the story is that one of the killers is dead, and no loss to society."

Most ravaging of the system's irrationalities was its racist aspects. The State of Mississippi, in a rare plunge into the realm of public relations, advertised in national magazines the virtues of a visit there. Featuring a photo of its Miss Hospitality, Loren Ormond, the ad read: "The romance and enchantment of antebellum days comes to life during Pilgrimage Time in Mississippi. Civil War battle sites, forts, monuments, shrines and museums make the Hospitality State a sightseer's paradise. Come enjoy fascinating Mississippi this spring." An enlightened son of the South, baseball's Alvin Dark, manager of Willie Mays, Willie McCovey, Orlando Cepeda and Juan Marichal, had this to say as he grappled with the issue of the day: "The majority of the people in the South, especially the Christian people that I have associated with, have really and truly liked the colored people. As for socializing with them on different levels there is a line drawn in the South, and I think it's going to be a number of years before this is corrected, or it may never be corrected. The way I feel, the colored boys who are baseball players are the ones I know best, and there isn't any of them that I don't like. When I first played with them on the Giant ball club . . . all these boys were, as far as I was concerned, wonderful boys and I never had any kind of trouble any way with them. I felt that because I was from the South—and we from the South actually take care of the colored people, I think, better than they're taken care of in the North—I felt when I was playing with them it was a responsibility for me. . . . There are a lot of people in the South that feel that everyone's a human being, a son of God, if they are Christians, all born equally. I feel that right now it's being handled a bit too fast. It's true that in a number of cases things have to be done in order to get something accomplished, things that might be a little fast for a certain community at this particular time. But I know that the majority of the Christian people in the South want to help any person who has Negro blood in them in any way possible because they feel like we are all born equal, we are all the sons of God and in the end will all be brothers in one faith. Being a Christian, I feel that this will be solved one day in the South. But they're rushing it a little bit too quick right now."

Boston brahmin Bobby Kennedy fared little better than Dixie's Dark. Testifying before the Senate Commerce Committee, RFK was asked by South Carolina's Strom Thurmond, "Would you say the Black Muslim movement is similar to the Nazi Party of the United States?" "No," replied the Attorney General liberally, "I think it is much closer to the Ku Klux Klan." Such insights from the head of the nation's Justice Department were enough to discourage the most misty-eyed Pollyanna. But *Ebony* magazine attempted to raise hopes. There are some thirty-five black millionaires in the United States, according to the journal, which speculated that there would be many more were it not for the conservatism of the black businessman. The magazine also contended that "obtaining capital has been a large obstacle for Negroes."

Only Ken Kesey, with assistance from Spike Milligan, might have dreamed up our next scene, the setting: Washington, D.C. In the Senate chamber, Florida's George Smathers was speaking against a civil rights bill. "How can you say you are protecting the black man when there are only five of you there?" interrupted a 26-year-old black man, from the spectator's gallery. "There are 20 million Americans who don't know what is going on here," continued Kenneth Washington of Passaic, New Jersey, as attendants began hustling him from the gallery. "There are 100 Senators and only five of them here and only two debating," he protested. "Apparently he is mentally disturbed," diagnosed Police Captain James Powell after questioning him. He could have been charged with disorderly conduct, Powell told the press, but was sent to the hospital for observation instead.

The racist aspect of U.S. capitalism is certainly its Achilles' heel. Can any nation keep its humanity intact when in one state, New York, twenty-one members of the Black Panther Party are arrested in an alleged bomb plot and held on $100,000 bail each; and in another state, Nebraska, a white police officer can admittedly shoot and kill a fourteen-year-old black girl, plead manslaughter, and be released the same day under $500 bond. Pathology permeates the U.S. Government without discrimination. Recently, CBS queried the U.S. embassy official in Saigon in charge of the refugee question on how he would characterize our program in Vietnam. Well, he answered, it should be seen as getting the people out of hostile Sioux country and into the safety of Fort Laramie. Which, for students of U.S. history, should answer any doubts still existing about the genocidal character of the American position in Vietnam.

That was a half-dozen years ago, 1963, when I was losing all those jobs. The massive March on Washington was the peak of a crescendo that began in Montgomery seven years before and reached a roar with the Birmingham demonstrations earlier that spring. Having just lost the poverty job, I drove east from California for the March. A quarter of a million people, black and white, was an impressive sight, but aside from the size of the gathering, there was little to stir about. Only two things occurred of lasting impact for me. John Lewis, chairman of the Student Non-Violent Coordinating Committee, was scheduled to speak. I had come to know John a bit through his trips to the West Coast and I was looking forward to his letting the good people know where things were at in the movement. He would tell them about Danville, Virginia, where SNCC organizers and townspeople had their heads and breasts split open six weeks earlier for demonstrating. And he'd talk about the nine leaders in Albany, Georgia, being prosecuted by Bobby Kennedy's Justice Department for alleged crimes which had been accepted as custom for a century when committed by whites. And about the three SNCC field workers facing the death penalty in Americus, Georgia, for "attempted insurrection." He was to declare, "We will march through the South, through the Heart of Dixie, the way Sherman did. We shall pursue our own 'scorched earth' policy and burn Jim Crow to the ground—nonviolently." And that SNCC couldn't "in good conscience" support the Administration's program of "too little, too late." That that program wouldn't give the vote to folks in Mississippi who lack a sixth grade education; that those who had a sixth grade education wouldn't be protected by a law administered by racist judges; that there was nothing in the civil rights bill to protect against police brutality. And that the party of Kennedy is also the party of Eastland, the party of Javits also the party of Goldwater, and he would ask, where is *our* party. John Lewis was going to say all this. But he never got the chance. He was allowed to say only the part of his speech approved by the Catholic archbishop, the United Auto Workers president and the executive director of the A. Phillip Randolph Foundation. The liberal establishment's college of cardinals had voted to protect the tender sensibilities of the politicians in residence a couple of blocks away. Whatever illusions marchers may have entertained around the reflecting pool that August day were shattered by the blast of bombs executing four teenage girls on Youth Day at the Sixteenth Street Baptist Church in Birmingham. And any admission of the validity of Malcolm's skepticism about the famous stroll through Washington's streets is recognition coming somewhat late in the day.

The other thing that sticks in my mind from that day is hearing the groans of 100,000 people gathered on the lawns of the Washington Monument as Emcee Ossie Davis announced that word had just arrived from Ghana that William E. B. DuBois was dead. The tears that fell that morning, and the sobs that racked the breasts of the Southern black people especially, were moving tribute to the memory of the man who may well have been our nation's most important genius of the 20th century, a memory that overcame twenty years of attempted blackout by the media, and that few outside of the Communist Party fought to maintain.

nine

Leroy Rivers plays it cool
Leroy Rivers don't study in school
Leroy Rivers smokes his Lark.
Leroy Rivers ain't nothing but dark.

—LEROY RIVERS, *Ninth grade,*
Ocean-Hill-Brownsville, N.Y.,
Experimental District

Civil rights had by now become the dominant issue in the student unrest, perhaps because it offered moral options with such pronounced clarity. And with the SNCC initiative in the South, being met head-on by the Wallaces and Faubuses, the underside of the Mason-Dixon became Shangri-la for newfound young people to exercise their moral choice. The move of young whites South has been interpreted as an act of atonement for guilt, and certainly there was such an element in the motives of many. In any case, there was the recognition that a crime had been and was being committed, and that these whites would no longer be part of the problem, as Eldridge Cleaver has put it, but wished to become part of the solution. Of course, with no historical sense nor collective consciousness, these students brought down in their knapsacks a good many new problems, which eventually brought the need for the assertion of black power.

When I returned to the Bay Area from Europe early in 1963, I found that Marxist discussion groups calling themselves W.E.B. DuBois Clubs had been set up in Berkeley and San Francisco, on the initiative of young Communists. The clubs had begun to issue a number of pamphlets—on Cuba, the Common Market, Vietnam. The last I found to be quite shabby and set myself the task of writing another. Madame Nhu the late, had announced her intention of visiting San Francisco and I wanted the pamphlet completed by her arrival. It made the points that the Vietnam war was a case of U.S. imperialist aggression (that it was "we" who invited the Diem regime into Vietnam, not the reverse); that the National Liberation Front was the legitimate representative of the South Vietnamese people; that the U.S. was about to massively increase its presence in that country; and that the alternative, the only correct one, was complete and immediate withdrawal. Causing a bit of controversy, coming as it did when even most people in the movement couldn't locate Vietnam on a map, it sold several thousand copies and became an organizing tool for the DuBois Clubs. By the time the Dragon Lady visited the Bay Area, we were able to prevent her peaceable assembly in Berkeley, and to organize a sit-in at her San Francisco hotel, forcing her to come and go by a secret entrance in a manner to which her sponsors in Washington soon were to become accustomed. The debut of the DuBois Clubs as an action organization was auspicious and, fancying our chances, we decided to have a go at the racist hiring practices of a number of business concerns.

Mels' Drive-In Restaurants, a Bay Area chain, was selected as the first target. Mels' Berkeley spot served as watering trough for Berkeley teenagers and motorcycle gangs, and as the one eatery open late enough to quench post-movie hunger. Of the couple-hundred employees in the chain, less than a dozen were black, and those worked at menial tasks. We began the campaign with picket lines, switching back and forth from the Berkeley restaurant to Oakland's to one or another in San Francisco. The sidewalk demonstrations, by their nature, slowed down business by causing traffic jams. What they also caused was aggravation to Mels' owner, Harold Dobbs. Dobbs, not incidentally, was running as the Republican candidate for mayor in San Francisco, his chances considered at least even. His opponent, Congressman John Shelley, had once been head of the city's Central Labor Council, and it was still from this body that he drew his main support. The campaign was perhaps the most tepid in San Francisco history. Columnist Herb Caen wrote, "you could safely bathe a baby in its gentle waters"—until the DuBois Clubs brought the waters to a boil.

Up to then, the issue of racism had been buried by both candidates by a gentlemen's agreement. Both stood four-square for compassion and understanding and things like that. But our demonstrations started to get to Dobbs. Older radical friends of the DuBois Clubs, together with allies in the labor movement and sympathizers in Shelley's campaign urged us to cool it, saying we were fucking over the congressman's chances. We argued that we were right on the issue, that Shelley shouldn't be mayor if he wasn't prepared to join us, that up to that point there seemed little choice between the candidates, and that, if anything, we were drawing the witless Dobbs out of his shell, giving folks someone to vote against, since they had no one to vote for. By now, we were bringing out several hundred pickets each night. We decided to increase the pressure: the Saturday before the election, we brought our demonstration to Dobbs' home in San Francisco's St. Francis Woods neighborhood, Waspish as a Radio City Music Hall comedy. This brought the candidate out swinging. "This, ladies and gentlemen," said Dobbs, "is what the people of San Francisco would face if Mr. Shelley were your mayor. No person's job would be safe. No person's home and family would be safe. No place of business in San Francisco would be allowed to conduct its business—and serve its customers—in an orderly way, without fear of threats and violence." Dobbs' outburst forced Shelley to come to our defense, with whatever little majesty he was able to muster. That night, we decided to frost our cake, moving into both the Berkeley and main San Francisco Mels' en masse with simultaneous sit-ins. In Berkeley, the place just closed down its business for the night; in San Francisco, police moved in to arrest a couple dozen of us. The next day, Sunday, 48 hours before the balloting, we repeated the action, with the same results: shut-down in Berkeley, some 50 arrests in San Francisco, the first mass arrests of civil rights demonstrators in the Bay Area. Arraignment day was also election day, and Harold Dobbs lost heavily. In the winning Democratic headquarters, unofficial word was a begrudging admission that the sit-ins were the deciding factor. For the first time in a generation, a Marxist movement was a major factor in the political life of an important American city.

Within a week, Harold Dobbs had signed an agreement with

our Ad-Hoc Committee to End Discrimination, adding dozens of black employees. We moved quickly to compound our victory. In the next fifteen days, we signed agreements with two other Bay Area chains, these without demonstrations. Then, we became momentarily paralyzed as events in Dallas took their course on November 22, less than three weeks after the San Francisco election. I was working at the time in a printshop as an apprentice bookbinder. The foreman came in to announce to the sixty employees that the President was dead, the victim of assassination, whereupon to a man and woman my shopmates glanced up, shook their heads in acknowledgement of the news and went back to work. Only one person commented at all, a woman sewing machine operator, who exclaimed, "Poor Jackie. First losing the baby, and now this." At the day's end, I hurried home to hear the news that the suspected assassin had been at one time in the past connected with Fair Play for Cuba. Everyone in the movement started calling, expressing fears of another Reichstag fire, and suggesting we lie low for awhile, taking care to lock our doors, and wait until the crunch comes or the heat blows over. The amazing thing about the mass reaction to the assassination was the gut suspicion of a conspiracy. That suspicion has since been bolstered by a number of studies of that day in Dallas, but what is telling about that assassination (and Malcolm's and Dr. King's) is that regardless of whether they were CIA conspiracies or not, millions of people assume that they were.

December saw the beginning of Ad-Hoc Committee negotiations with San Francisco's Sheraton-Palace Hotel. The most narcissistic city in the nation, priding itself in its liberalism at a level approaching preciousness, contained perhaps the most racist hotel industry in the 50 states. In Birmingham hotels, black bartenders and waiters are commonplace, but in San Francisco that year there were none. The city's hostelries were in a vulnerable position, all of them booked several months in advance to play host to the Republican National Convention. The Sheraton-Palace, soon to be Rockefeller headquarters, employed nineteen blacks, all in menial jobs, of a work staff totaling 550. Testimony by Howard Jewel, aide to the state attorney general, four months after our negotiations began, revealed that efforts a year earlier by the Fair Employment Practices Commission to determine the racial composition of the Sheraton-Palace had failed because of rebuffs from the hotel.

Our talks, coming on the heels of the Mels' Drive-In victory, seemed to elicit more response than was accorded the FEPC. Spokesmen for the hotel, after a couple of sessions, released the figures cited above but said they were moving with dispatch to improve the situation. In the next two months of our discussions, twelve more black workers were hired, including one auditor, one bartender and several shoeshine men, less than adequate at best. When we pressed the point, the city's Hotel Association, representing the 35 major inns, joined the Sheraton-Palace management at the next meeting, at which we were told in quite certain terms to push off. We set up a picket line two nights later. This was February 23, 1964. What happened from there on in could serve as a primer on how city fathers deal when pushed to the wall. We were called into another meeting with the Hotel Association and threatened with an injunction if we didn't call off our brigades. That night, we took on the Sheraton again, this time entering the hotel through one door and exiting through another, a perpetual human locomotive chugging through the lobby, with field representatives of San Francisco's Red Squad looking on. After a bit of this, the injunction was presented. Calling the train to a halt, we took a vote and decided for the moment to leave the hotel. The next night, a Sunday, we invited Dick Gregory down from his club to join us, along with local NAACP and CORE leaders. The injunction was still in effect, but this time we chose to ignore it. Several sides of beef, wearing the uniform of the SFPD, came along to bust us. One hundred and seven of us spent the night in jail before bail came.

We sent out the call for a mass defiance of the injunction to be demonstrated the following Friday evening. The leader of our movement was a very beautiful eighteen-year-old woman, Tracy Sims, unequalled as a mass leader in the Bay Area until Huey P. Newton began the Black Panther Party. The heat was on Tracy and a few others of us for the next few days, so we made ourselves scarce while drawing up contingency plans for Good Friday. New injunctions were handed down limiting our pickets to less than 100, denying us permission to enter the hotel or block doorways, or to "conspire" to do any of these dastardly deeds. The Hotel Association revealed to the press the startling information that Dr. DuBois joined the Communist Party late in life, thereby shedding light on who we were. Local headhunters, writing columns for the city's gazettes, followed up by printing unexpurgated and un-abridged slices of the pornography that passes as reports to Congress from HUAC, these paying special tribute to the past exploits of myself and a few friends. Mayor Shelley announced that he doubted the sincerity of the demonstrators; and Governor Brown, who had by now mastered the rudimentaries of the smear, demonstrated his capacities in the field.

The United San Francisco Freedom Movement, containing every established civil rights organization in town, came to our defense, letting it be known that we received its unreserved support. The local CORE chairman blasted the red-baiting as a device to divide friends in a fight against a common enemy. Local union support, particularly from the longshoremen, was solicited. And *The East Bay Labor Journal,* the voice of Alameda County's AFL-CIO, hailed our fight against "private enterprise's" incursions on "human rights" and suggested a comparison to the labor sit-downs a quarter-century before. We let it be known that there would be no loyalty oaths on the picket line and organized a turnout from San Jose to Sacramento. About 3,000 showed up to defy the injunction, facing the wrath of the several hundred pigs and horses in attendance. Earlier in the week, the Hotel Association said that it was "prepared to discuss our employment practices with any responsible group or state agency, but not under threats of picketing, boycotting, violence or other means of coercion." Up to the day of the demonstration, it made constant appeals for some "responsible group" to come forward and repudiate us, but no one showed up at its Nilene testing station. Even as we gathered outside, the management hadn't run out of arguments. A group of us were called in to the executive offices and told that the proposed agreement violated their collective bargaining contracts and the unions would not allow them to sign. A few phone calls to the unions themselves repudiated this contention. Against the best advice of some our civic leader "friends" who said they couldn't help us with bail, we went outside to invite our other friends into the hotel lobby. More than a thousand of them.

And there we remained. For nineteen hours. More than 200 of us were busted in the course of the night, the rest doing what comes natural to a hotel environment—going to sleep. At three P.M. the next day, a limousine pulled up the drive to take Tracy and a few more of us to see the mayor. Waiting in his offices were San Francisco's leading clergy, white and black, a number of trade union officials, and the lawyers for the Hotel Association. They had copies of a document which they asked us to peruse to see if it met with our approval. We were so spent of energy and emotion, it took several minutes to grasp the fact that we had won. Not only at the Sheraton-Palace but throughout the Hotel Association's 35 member hotels. In the next year, they were to hire 1,500 black and Chicano workers in all categories. We had won 1,500 jobs plus the right to tour all hotels at any time to guarantee the agreement was being observed.

Whatever fire was directed at us prior to the agreement now

reached proportions of white heat, as it were. Media spokesmen, captains of industry and government officials all began genuflecting at the sight of a policeman's billy and sounded the catechism of law and order. Typical was the reaction of the lead political writer in San Francisco's *Examiner:* "As I watched the Palace Hotel disturbances I was moved to disgust and anger—but beyond these emotions to a deep sense of anguish. . . . What emerged from the Palace demonstrations was a tenuous bridgehead for *an alien thought.* There was official, semi-official and private recognition of government by mob. . . . It was my basic rights to a government by law they were kicking around—at the Palace and at the conference table. The signed agreement is an outlaw pact. It is a contract between nobody and nobody about nothing. . . . There is the propaganda attempt by the agitators to equate the hotel agreement with the collective bargaining contracts arrived at in lawful negotiations between unions and employers. . . . The hotel document can more fairly be compared with the strictly illegal undertaking of a harassed shopkeeper to pay 'protection' money to a terror gang. . . . As for the mob itself, it was allowed to do collectively at the Palace what any Third Street bum would have been jugged for doing, had he tried it on a whim. . . . Law, law, law! Always the emphasis on orderly procedure so that in protecting the legal rights of minorities we did not undermine the structure of our society of law. Now the arrival of the agitators, some of them Marxist-oriented, and the law that protects us all is desecrated. From here it would seem to be up to the Negro community to choose its friends, the old or the new. They can't have it both ways." The paper itself editorialized that "the enormously dangerous aspect of the lawlessness by young black and white zealots has been its success. . . . It worked and they got away with it, not only enthroning lawlessness as a civil rights weapon but dethroning responsible civil rights leaders in favor of reckless militants."

A few courageous souls took exception to the hysteria. Satirist Arthur Hoppe wrote in *The Chronicle* of an earlier demonstration which violated conservative concepts of law and order, including incursions on private property, and whose tactics at the time were decried as outrageous and disgraceful. The circumstances: the night of December 16, 1773, after a meeting in the Old South Church, 40 or 50 revolutionaries went down to Boston harbor, boarded three British ships and dumped overboard 342 chests of tea. "Since, of course, they have all been enshrined in the pantheon of American heroes." And *The Peoples World* pointed out that there was now more scurrying about in City Hall and private business to "do something" about this problem than in all past decades.

When, a week after the Sheraton victory, over 100 of us were busted as we took on San Francisco's automobile row, the mayor summoned us to his offices to tell us he was setting up a Human Relations Commission which would be bringing suits against racist employers. *The Chronicle* summed up the Mayor's dilemma: "Shelley tried to persuade the traditional, responsible, Negro leadership to repudiate the new civil disobedience tactics employed by Michael Myerson and Tracy Sims, leaders of the newly formed Ad Hoc Committee. He privately admits he failed in this effort. Shelley learned that responsible Negroes, for the most part are unwilling publicly to disavow a tactic that proved spectacularly successful. The thrust of Shelley's efforts then switched to what he called, 'the realities of the situation.' He is now convinced the civil rights fight in San Francisco is well organized at the top, and is following a definite pattern. No matter how much he might wish it were not true, the Ad Hoc Committee is part of it. 'In the Lucky Stores,' he said, 'it was CORE that nominally fronted for the demonstration. In the Sheraton-Palace it was the Ad Hoc Committee. With Cadillac it is the NAACP. And in each case it was the Ad Hoc Committee that supplied the troops.' " The newly formed Human Relations Commission soon got agreement from the automobile dealers to change their ways. New voices of outrage were heard when the media reported a top official saying that we had "touched a raw nerve in the power structure" and I responded that our goal was to give that structure a nervous breakdown. This was final proof of our seditious intent.

We said at the time that the days for neutrality on the issue of racist oppression were gone; that today neutrality was by default a racist position. To charges of irresponsibility, we showed that we had negotiated with the hotel industry for two and a-half months before we began demonstrations; that at each stage it was the hotels that broke off negotiations, including on the last night of demonstrations, that everyone from the Mayor to former U. S. Secretary of Labor James Mitchell acknowledged this; that the hotels had been discriminatory for half a century and making promises to change for fifteen years, that those promises could never feed hungry families, and it was therefore the hotels and industry that were irresponsible.

We argued that the indignant outcries came because we had won 1,500 new jobs for people of color; that this was no abstract brotherhood week where the flag is hoisted and a new school named for Booker T. Washington. As a result of our acts, every opponent of the movement all of a sudden came out in favor of the movement, only opposed "the tactics." For the first time, scores of news columnists, businessmen, government officials, announced they were for picket lines, saying pickets are a legitimate form of protest, unlike sit-ins. These were people who only two weeks earlier sought or supported the injunction to stop our picket line; none of those new picket line proponents were around when ten days before, the Sheraton-Palace got their injunction limiting our demonstration to nine pickets. Which is not unlike more recent speeches by these same "leaders" harking back with nostalgia to those days of nonviolence as setting the correct path for our movement today.

I recall President Eisenhower in early 1960, being asked about the recent sit-downs in the South to achieve equal eating privileges, replying "I am not lawyer enough or wise enough in this area to know when such a matter is such as actually to violate the constitutional right of the Negroes," and asking that the sit-inners consider peaceful marches as a more desirable form of demonstration. A short seven years later, we had "progressed" to the stage where *The New York Times* could report, "Secretary of Defense Robert S. McNamara directed today that military personnel who wish to enter civilian police work be given early discharges as part of an effort to strengthen police forces in the major cities."

Police chiefs all across the country were socially weaned on *National Geographic* rotogravures of Polynesians, spears in hand, wearing loin cloths. The specter of these people is still conjured up in their darkest moments, only the .38 has replaced the spear and the black leather jacket the loin cloth. In the chiefs' minds the word "savages" remains the same. And we have now arrived at the point in every major city, when the morning herald reports as a daily occurence, the cop on the beat firing half a dozen "warning" shots into the head and abdomen of the kid with the black beret. It makes one long for the old days of the peaceable cop, serviced only by the billy and the black jack, his tools of the trade.

A couple of months after the automobile row, and then the Bank of America, campaigns, the Ad Hoc Committee decided to spread its favors around the Bay Area, choosing as its new target the Oakland *Tribune*, that city's only daily newspaper. Oakland, for years reputed as the armpit of the nation, was seen by *Tribune* owner William Knowland as his personal fief. To take on the newspaper was to avoid the middleman, to shoot for the head.

After months of negotiations with the man, we began our demonstrations. During our talks we learned only that Mr. Knowland possessed an encyclopedic knowledge of the trivial; our demonstration brought out his other paramount trait—a mammoth incapacity to tolerate incursions on his fiefdom. Two things happened in quick succession to end the Ad Hoc Committee. First came a division in our ranks over tactics; a minority wished to sit in immediately, the majority to gradually escalate tactics to the point of massive confrontation. One day, during a demonstration, ten of the former decided they were going to block *The Tribune* gates. One of our leaders, Mark Comfort, and I argued against this, they went ahead anyway, so we moved our troops down the block away from the sit-in. A few moments after the ten were arrested, Inspector Charles Gain, today chief of police of that fair city, busted Mark and me on a variety of charges, all beginning with "aiding and abetting." The split in our committee became irreconcilable and eventually resulted not only in its demise but in the ten sit-inners receiving ten-days-suspended sentences, and Mark and I two six-month sentences, nonsuspended, justice from which I remain fugitive today. Simultaneous with these occurrences, was pressure by Knowland on the University of California to stop letting its premises be used as recruiting grounds for outside agitators operating in Oakland. It was this pressure that first brought the heat down on our people at the university's Sather Gate entrance, resulting spontaneously in what would become the 1964 Free Speech Movement. The FSM of course overshadowed all other movement efforts at the time, and *The Tribune* campaign ended abruptly and unsuccessfully. The elders of the tribe had pause to smile.

That year, 1964, was the Year of the Nazi. In Washington, Attorney General Robert Kennedy authorized the sale of General Aniline and Film, a very valuable property once owned by I. G. Farben, back, in part, to the Swiss company which served as the dummy for I. G. Farben. It was Farben that had used Auschwitz slave labor. For the 20 years since the war, all attorneys general held to a policy that General Aniline and Film should not be reverted to Farben. Drew Pearson allowed as how Bobby Kennedy's reversal of previous policy might be explained by the fact that General Aniline vice chairman was William Payton Martin, "legal counsel of Joseph P. Kennedy and family; general counsel for the Joseph P. Kennedy enterprises," according to *Who's Who*. Farben wasn't alone in its return to power. Krupp's total sales that year approached five billion marks, about four times that of 1943 at the height of the war. Alfred Krupp, back at the helm, had been sentenced at Nuremberg to twelve years in prison for his company's wartime use of slave labor. He was freed two and a half years later, with U. S. High Commissioner John J. McCloy finding reasonable doubt he was responsible for the policies of a company "in which he occupied a rather junior position," this despite the fact that Alfred ran the Krupp enterprises the last two years of the war. A similar tough policy was in force in 1964, as Adolf Eichmann's top aide, Hermann Krumey was sentenced to five years at hard labor for complicity in the murder of at least 300,000 Hungarian Jews of the 437,000 he deported to Auschwitz; Krumey's co-defendant, former SS Captain Otto Hunsche, was acquitted of the same charges. Meanwhile, in Heidenheim an der Brenz, hundreds of Afrika Korps veterans paid tribute to Field Marshal Erwin Rommel, three days before the 20th anniversary of the death of the Desert Fox. And in Rendsburg, the eleventh annual SS rally took place. The Waffen-SS, condemned by the allied war crimes tribunals as a criminal body, holds its annual rally as a welfare organization representing the interests of and providing funds for the dependents of deceased comrades, not unlike New York's Policeman's Benevolent Association. What was impressive about all this nostalgia for atrocity, was the constant news reports of a parade of U. S. Congressmen and Senators traveling to or wiring greetings to right-wing rallies in Germany. Although it might be seen as an appropriate follow-up to President Kennedy's "Ich bin ein Berliner" speech the year before. Meanwhile congressional hands were wrung and eyes teared at the mention of the Berlin Wall.

General Barry Goldwater had won his sought-after nomination. Never having attended a Klan rally nor a police chief's convention, even my newly jaundiced mind boggled at those San Francisco proceedings which caused the Governor of California to remark that "the stench of fascism is in the air." Only the month before, the city council of Albany, the town adjacent to Berkeley, upheld the rejection of Cecil Thomas from its Civil Service Board because he was "too controversial." A Quaker, Cecil had been a key advisor, through his job at the university YMCA, to SLATE in its early days, and was one of the sweetest persons I'd ever met. The incidents that made him "too controversial" were his arrest in Jackson, Mississippi, in 1961 when he entered a coffee shop in the company of a black friend, and his participation in a disarmament demonstration in Las Vegas in 1957. Governor Brown, whose nostrils detected "the stench of fascism" at the Goldwater convention, must have had a head cold the day Cecil lost his job, or else the postal service from Sacramento broke down that week, but nary a protest was heard from that quarter.

And, in Atlantic City, the other guys were riding herd for Johnson's renomination, as the Mississippi Freedom Democrats were nearly trampled to death. In November, 26 million citizens exercised their prerogative by voting for "the stench of fascism." The balance of the vote went for Lyndon Johnson. Of course, it can be placed in the I-told-you-so category, but a few of us curious types who were premature in wondering what 25,000 "special advisers" were doing in Vietnam, warned that the Tonkin fraud that August was a bit of a tip-off as to what to expect after election day. In 1964 there was a good deal of worry by those leading the presidential charade about the immorality of American youth, and the need to show us the path to redemption. Their pointing was in itself enough to make us take a left turn, against instructions.

In the spring of that year, heady with our success in the Bay Area, the DuBois Clubs decided to go national. I was dispatched around the country to recruit people for a founding national convention to be held in June in San Francisco. The gathering brought together about 600 people and was keynoted by the Reverend Milton Galamison of New York. Except when we broke to demonstrate at the local Hilton where President Johnson was staying—to my knowledge, the first confrontation he encountered over his Vietnam aggression—the convention was for the most part uneventful. (Though it should be mentioned that we became the first U.S. organization to give formal unreserved support to South Vietnam's NLF.) The three days were consumed by an ongoing floor fight between delegates from the Progressive Labor Party and Bay Area Du Boisniks, a forerunner by half a dozen years to the convention that saw the division of Students for a Democratic Society. Floor leader for PL was Philip Abbot Luce, who later reported on the convention in his book, *The New Left*, and in testimony before congressional committees in his capacity as paid informer. Luce became a prostitute, sure enough, his going rate $1,000 a day, according to Ohio congressman Wayne Hays. In his book, Luce gives credit for the "invaluable research help provided" to Herb Rommerstein. Apparently Luce's procurer, Rommerstein is the FBI operative, mentioned earlier in regard to my youth festival days. *Reporter* magazine, reviewing *The New Left*, acclaims Luce as "another Whittaker Chambers," and is cheered because the author didn't have to wait until his life was almost over to see the errors of his ways. Like flies gathering around a pile of dung, the critics paid homage to the new Luce.

Within a year and a half after the founding convention, most of us who had been most instrumental in its formation left the organization over policy questions, a split from which the clubs never really recovered. It was a time when SDS was just becoming a mass student organization, when it subscribed to concepts of "counter-community" and "participatory democracy." Many within SDS and also the DuBois Clubs saw us as competing organizations, a view which I resisted. The two served quite different purposes, with varying constituencies, and neither was about to take state power; we had everything to gain from cooperation, I believed. Fundamental to their differences was the fact that the DuBois Clubs were socialist, SDS at the time antipathetic to any ideology. One of the more enthralling ironies is the claims of revolutionary Communism by most of SDS today, and the embracing of Stalin by some, both cardinal sins that they accused us of back then. A common assumption by most observers then was that it was an age of modest comfort, that economic protests were passé, that being comfortable materially, the students' dissatisfactions were of a spiritual and moral nature. It is a middle class rebellion, they said, an assumption that we rejected, at least insofar as we were concerned. One argument against us, as being "old left" and undemocratic was that we would organize people into organizations in which we had a program; it was democratic, such critics felt, only to organize people into organizations without a program. It flowed from this that we should organize people into *their* own organizations, but not into *ours*. I remember an impromptu discussion between a DuBois slum kid and a student from one of the SDS projects. The latter suggested that in order to learn from one another, it might be a good idea to exchange people. "We'll send you a couple of organizers from our project to your project and you send some of your people to us." The DuBois kid was hard put to explain that he had no "project," that he was in a club, that the other members were his friends, not his subjects.

A number of myths were created about both SDS and the DuBois Clubs in those days. Jack Newfield, formerly an SDS member, was typical of inflicting injury of this sort. Drawing pretty hard and fast lines, Newfield included in his "new left," not only SDS and SNCC, but also the Peace Corps and Timothy Leary. This was counterposed to the "hereditary left" like PL and the DuBois Clubs. Newfield's new left grew up during the years of "Warsaw, Auschwitz, Hiroshima, Nuremburg, Seoul and Budapest," the implication being that the "hereditary left" reached puberty in Petrograd. The latter is "oriented toward either China or the Soviet Union rather than toward forging a new vision of American society," wrote Newfield. Aside from the slur on the hundreds of young Americans who also had gone to jail, been beaten and framed by cops in order to build a new America, Newfield's point was decidedly dangerous. For while opposing McCarthyism, he himself wielded its cutting edge, the foreign ideology myth. He spoke of the "alien cobwebbed dogmas of Marx, Lenin, and Trotsky" followed by his heditary left, as opposed to his new left's adherence to the "existential humanism of Camus" and the "anti-colonialism of Fanon," those two great U.S. nationals.

Newfield tried to define the difference between the DuBois Clubs and SDS. "DuBois members are just not 'hung-up' by the same things SDSers are. They don't talk about feeling powerless against managerial bureaucracies. They don't make embarrassing speeches about how we must love each other." Ready for the key difference? "The key difference is that DuBois Club members don't hate their fathers; SDSers do." In fact, the main difference aside from the socialism of the DuBois Clubs, such as it was, was that they did not see themselves as "middle-class." I remember a conversation with a former SDS national president during Berkeley's gigantic Vietnam Day teach-in. I was to be on a midnight panel with this friend in a discussion of the new left. I begged out and got Carl Bloice, a close comrade, to take my place. The next day I asked my SDS friend how the panel went. He said it was okay but at one point he had to take Carl to task. I asked why that was and he replied that Carl, a young black man, said that one of the most exciting moments of his life was meeting a representative of the South Vietnam National Liberation Front in Europe. I asked the SDS leader, "And how did you disagree?" "Well, I told him that the most exciting moment of my life was meeting 'Mrs. Smith down on D Street.'" I had to point out to him that aside from being a patronizing schmuck, he should know that Carl had lived with "Mrs. Smith on D Street" all of his life.

Saul Landau and Paul Jacobs wrote in their book, *The New Radicals,* by far the best of the spate of works published at the time, that "It was SDS that injected economics into the early civil rights movement, and underlined the role of private American capitalism in supporting foreign as well as American racism." Of course, older leftists had done this for 40 years. It is not that SDS was wrong; on the contrary, it was the heir to a tradition that is the best in American history. It was certainly correct, but it did not understand that its forebears were also right. Landau and Jacobs wrote that "the rejection of Marxism, the only ideology that revolutionaries have had for a hundred years, placed an enormous burden on the shoulders" of SDS. They might have added that Marxism remains today the ideology for the millions of revolutionaries from Cuba to Vietnam, from Spain to the Philippines. And to reject it was indeed a heavy burden. The two writers prophetically concluded their book by writing: "The new radicals do not and will not give adequate or convincing answers to the Communist question. . . . They are correct in refusing the stale arguments and acrimony of past quarrels but they cannot avoid an ideological confrontation with the Communist position in the sixties. . . . But few young radicals are sure of themselves in terms of ideology. They feel much more secure in postures of moral intransigence, using the purity of youth and action to answer their critics' political attacks. To them Communism is an issue raised only by those over 30, therefore they need not be concerned with it. . . . And yet the concern with the here and now, the emphasis on action and the moral witness are the very reason that so many Movement projects deteriorate. Enthusiasm can carry one only a short distance before a more substantial fuel is required. . . . The questions for the new radicals are whether they are going to work out a more coherent ideology; whether they are willing to commit themselves to jail but not to 20 or 30 years of difficult political effort."

For those of us who came to Marxism early in the student movement it is exciting to see so many thousands reject the *X* and *R* ratings given that body of thought by the education factories. (Although, it might be appropriate to confer on it an *M*, "for mature audiences only.") Enormous tasks confront those approaching Marxism: the avoidance of sectarianism, of bureaucracy and manipulation, of self-centeredness as the only arbiters of the truth; the devising of a strategy to win the people of our country to the need for revolution; the building of a leadership party, whose base is working people, black and white. Cuban friends have told me that taking power was the easier part of the revolution; things got truly difficult after, when they tried to solve the incredible problems of underdevelopment. For us, at this point in our political lives, the coming to accept socialist thought has, for all the obstacles in the way, been the easy part. The difficulties are really beginning only now.

ten

"There's something on the other side of that
wall that has never been conquered."
"What's that?"
"Did you ever hear of Kong? That's why I
brought along the gas bombs."
                —Dialogue from King Kong

From the plethora of vices available to a young North American, I seem to have chosen the movies to wallow in. My all-time favorite, judging by the criteria of having viewed it eleven times, is *Casablanca*. Everyone's got lines they have singled out for special recall; the most famous is Bogart turning to Dooley Wilson and in drunken pain spurting: "Play it, Sam. If she can stand it, so can I," followed by Wilson's rendition of "As Time Goes By." I've got a different choice: Ingrid Bergman looking into Paul Henreid's eyes and pleading, "Darling, please don't go to the meeting of the underground tonight." The romance of it all does me in every time.

And the line kept bouncing around my mind that day in August 1965 as I boarded the plane to Hanoi. It had been quite a summer. Touring England speaking at anti-U.S. teach-ins, representing not-so-ugly America. Then the world peace assembly in Helsinki, where I first met the Vietnamese, both from the Front and the North, flattered to the skies being told they knew of my pamphlet on the war written two years earlier, and being asked to visit North Vietnam in the first group of Yankees since the 1954 Geneva Accords, save those shot uninvited from the skies. All of *Casablanca*'s intrigue and romance came back to me, as I made plans for the visit. There were so many uncertainties. After all, it was wartime, my country was bombing theirs, who could tell what might happen on returning to the States.

The arrangement was that I was to be in Paris on a certain day a month later when word would come regarding visas and flight. The determining factor would be the military situation in the North, *i.e.* how dangerous it might be for us, what with the U.S. bombing attacks on the increase. I spent that month traveling in the Soviet Union. Then I was on my way to Turkey, with an overnight stop in Greece, when my wallet with all papers and money was lifted in Athens. I camped on the doorstep of the U.S.

embassy trying to get a new passport. The local police were of no help, tied up at the time keeping the Athenians in line since, the week before, the King had removed Prime Minister George Papandreou, preliminary to the King's own removal by the colonel's coup two years later. After making of myself a general menace to the numerous attachés I encountered, the embassy finally gave me a new passport, which was to be itself lifted shortly, this time by the State Department for my trip to Hanoi. The night I got the passport, I went down to make my reservations to leave Athens. Coming out of the airlines office I saw police applying their version of a physical education to some young demonstrators, part of a throng of several thousand. Nothing is so painful to the ears and the stomach as the sound of the thud of a billy club on the head, and I moved in to stop the noise. The cop turned on me to place me under arrest, when he was hit from behind. I took off, through the crowd, back to my hotel, and out to the airport. Jail, even for one night, has always sent me up the walls and I wasn't interested in comparing the Greek product with those made in the USA. Especially when, that week, the Athens newspapers were full of a story about a bomb explosion some months before which killed a dozen Greeks and had now been discovered to have been set by the CIA to throw blame on local Communists.

Two weeks after leaving Greece, I was aboard the 28-seat, Soviet-built plane, filled to capacity. The passengers were all diplomats and technicians: Soviets, Bulgarians, Germans, Vietnamese, Chinese, Indonesian and Malian. There were four Americans, a New York radio journalist, a free-lance writer living in Paris, and two of us from San Francisco. After three days of plane hops from Paris to Warsaw to Moscow to Omsk and Irkutsk in Siberia to Peking, we began the final leg of our trip, a fifteen-hour prop flight to Hanoi. A brief stop was necessary 100 miles north of the Vietnam border before sundown, to check the landing security at that hour, since U.S. planes had recently conducted a series of bombing raids at dusk. The skies were clear, and we made the one-hour flight in peace. We were greeted upon our arrival in Hanoi by embraces and flowers, customary for guests of the socialist countries, presented to us by three young women of more than customary beauty, students of the faculty of medicine at the University of Hanoi. Also present were the leaders of the Vietnam Youth Federation, our hosts for the stay, and Nguyen Trung Hieu and Do Xuan Oanh of the Vietnamese Peace Committee, our friends from the Helsinki meeting, and from whom our invitation was secured. The day was very warm, the humidity high, and, in the suits and ties we wore as properly befits arriving guests, we perspired uncomfortably. Ho Truc, the Youth Federation's secretary-general, approached me as we walked toward the terminal. Wearing sport shirt and sandals, as were all his comrades, and noticing our discomfort, he explained to me: "You know, Mi Ko [my name for the visit, as pronounced by the monosyllabic Vietnamese], our people lived under colonial domination for a long long time and we are really a young country and new at governing ourselves. So we don't know a great deal about diplomacy and protocol, and [voice lowered to a whisper, accompanied by a wink] we really care about it even less. So take off your tie, wear what you wish, speak frankly as you like, and let us be brothers. This is your home." We had, at last, arrived in Vietnam, and the tone was set for our stay.

As was to be our fate for much of the following two weeks, we were driven to our hotel in a Zim, the ugly though luxurious Soviet limousine. We protested this special treatment, saying we felt like colonials, but were told in effect: Look, this is our country, we run it. This is how we treat our guests. If you feel like a colonial, that's your own problem. Relax and enjoy yourself. Life is too valuable to waste it on such hang-ups.

Hanoi was a lovely city of French colonial architecture, tree-lined streets and spacious lakes. The streets were filled, the masses, as they say, teeming. Ninety percent of all traffic was by bicycle; what motorized vehicles that existed were camouflaged. The city life was a paradox, military fortifications placed throughout in preparation for attack, and simultaneously a great effort was made to normalize existence. Everywhere, at the lakes, across bridges, at the university, government buildings and factories, antiaircraft fortifications were visible. At dawn and dusk, dozens of young people walked with rifles and camouflage to and from militia practice. At the same time, no curfew existed and there were no air-raid drills. There are two main tasks of the Vietnamese people, we were told over and over again: defend against the aggressors, and continue to construct socialism.

The morning after our arrival we met first with the leadership of the Youth Federation. The federation's building during the resistance war against the French served as the French Officer's Club, and it was from here that French operations at Dien Bien Phu were directed. After the 1954 settlement, the federation was offered its choice of buildings in recognition of its contributions to the resistance. The officers' club, one of Hanoi's grandest mansions, was ideal. Today, it stood directly across the street from France's diplomatic mission. "A perfect example of peaceful coexistence between peoples of different social systems," said Truc, with his ironic smile.

Of the DRV's seventeen million population, we were told, 700,000 are members of the Workers' (Communist) Party. The party has the greatest prestige because, since 1931, Communists have earned the respect of the people as nationalists through their leadership in the revolution and the resistance. Life prior to independence was one of illiteracy, ignorance and hunger. During the years of World War II alone, two million died of hunger, more than four times the combined total of U.S. dead in both world wars. In the past, three or four hundred thousand died each year of hunger and disease. Now, there is a yearly population increase approaching half a million. One of the Youth Federation's responsibilities is providing birth control education. Prior to the revolution, they tell us, it was not uncommon for teenage girls to have two or three children. Where before a man could have several wives and many children, there is now monogamy. The minimum age for marriage is 18, but young people are encouraged to postpone marriage. With 90 percent illiteracy prior to the revolution, landlords were able to steal the property and wives of the peasants through paperwork manipulation. By 1958, four years after the Geneva Agreements, complete literacy had been achieved on an elementary level. The first task of the revolution was to provide universal education. In 1939, the most prosperous year under the French, there were only 500 university students throughout Indochina. Now, there were 27,000 university students in North Vietnam alone. Before, the only subject taught was French law (to train colonial bureaucrats), now there were 20,000 scientific, technical, medical and engineering students. Along with the universal education of children, more than one million adults were attending evening school. And the government now boasted of having 85,000 teachers.

Malaria and cholera had disappeared in the North for all practical purposes. Mosquito nets for protection at night were now readily available. Peace is absolutely necessary, we were told, to build the good life. Socialism, they say, is based on a peacetime economy; war, aside from its destruction of human beings and land, puts a terrible strain in the economy. This they contrast to our capitalist economy that bases itself on war production and the plundering of other lands. But while peace is cherished and necessary, they tell us, the people of Vietnam are determined to have national independence. Peace and independence are synonymous. Any discussions that may take place had to have as their basis an acceptance of the national independence, sovereignty and unity of Vietnam, free from outside interference. To this end the Vietnamese people have literally dedicated their lives. And, said our friend Oanh in his sweet musician's voice, "the word 'defeat' cannot be found in the Vietnamese lexicon."

The war had naturally changed the nature of the Youth Federation. To meet the demanded changes, an appeal to the young people had been issued, just prior to our visit. Following discussions throughout the various organizations at every level, in the schools, factories, and villages, over two million young volunteers came forth to serve in the war. Many of the letters from volunteers are written in blood, as if there were further need to demonstrate their determination and commitment. Women volunteer equally with men. Young children pack their pockets with rocks, increasing their weight so as to be acceptable to the army.

After our meeting, outside the Federation offices, I chided Truc for the fact that no women were present among the youth leaders we had met. As a matter of coincidence, he replied, President Ho had criticized him for the same thing just the week before. "You cannot walk with one foot," said the venerable [their adjective] President, "or certainly not as quickly as is necessary. You must use both feet." Back in New York a month later, I thought of this comment, when I spotted a *Times* ad for the movie "Alfie," quoting from *Life:* "You are going to enjoy 'Alfie' very much. 'Alfie' uses people—mainly women—and throws them away like tissues."

One evening, we toured the city with its French colonnades, market places and ancient pagodas, many of which were bombed by the French just before their final retreat. We walked under the stars through Reunification Park, sprawling with palms surrounding its lake. We spoke in hushed whispers so as not to disturb the dozens of young couples curled up on the lake's bank, engrossed in each other's love. The park, Hieu tells us, was built entirely by young people and serves as the surrounding landscape for the new Polytechnic Institute which was also being built, with some Soviet aid, by the students and faculty of the school. One concept your government had better understand, he tells us, is that the schools have been built by the students and belong to them; they are not the property of boards of regents. Similarly, the factories were built by and belong to the workers who toil in them; they do not belong to any boards of directors. And the people are ready to give their lives to defend that which they have built. "This is part of our socialist consciousness," says Hieu.

One day we were privileged to meet Tran Thi Ly (in Vietnam, women often have the middle name Thi, or sister), one of Vietnam's national heroines. Sister Ly was a native of a village near Da Nang, adjacent to the large U.S. air base in the South. In the years 1956–57, she witnessed many tortures against her compatriots, a common experience for peasants in Diem's "bastion of democracy." Children were torn in two by their legs; pregnant women were used for target practice; draft evaders were disemboweled. Every day, Sister Ly would find bodies of children and villagers floating in the river near her home. She was moved to write a letter to the International Control Commission, set up by the Geneva Agreements, asking to testify as a witness to crimes against the village population. Five days later, Sister Ly was arrested, and for the next two years underwent constant torture. She was hung by her arms from the ceiling with electrodes applied to her breasts and vagina; bamboo stakes were shoved up her vagina; burning irons were shoved into her skin and twisted; for days at a time, she was buried up to her neck in excrement. After two years of torture, liberation front guerrillas freed her and she was brought North. She was sent for periods of medical treatment to the Soviet Union and China, but to this day she still required regular blood transfusions because of loss of blood from the vagina. Her nervous system was shot and she could not always retain consciousness. It had been eight years since her arrest when we met her. She was 26 years old.

Sister Ly was brought from the hospital to the Youth Federation offices for our visit. The meeting, one of the very few she had been able to make, was arranged at her request. It was difficult to believe at first that this strikingly beautiful woman seated with us, in her flowing white formal gown, could have suffered such punishment. But when the neck clips of her gown were unfastened we could see the horrible blotches of twisted flesh from severe burns and beatings, in horrifying contrast to the soft beauty of her face and the quiet tenderness of her voice. Not long after Sister Ly's arrest, her mother was arrested also. She had learned that her mother's back was broken, and she was presumably dead. Now, her two sisters, 23 and eighteen years old, remained in South Vietnamese prisons, along with 400,000 of their fellows. We were moved to silence, and sat holding hands with this national heroine, about whom many poems and songs had been written. The meeting ended, as she had to return to the hospital. It was Sister Ly who broke the quiet. "Please send my regards to all our progressive American friends. We have no ill feelings toward the American people. While we hate the imperialists, we hold in high regard the peace movement in your country and the sacrifices you have made on our behalf. Please tell this to your people for me."

People we encountered in the North saw their primary task as building the material base for socialism even while they repelled bombing and strafing attacks. Students played a special role because schools had become, along with hospitals, prime targets. Shortly before we arrived, the Pedagogical University had suffered serious bombings, with dozens of children perishing. Schools were now, like the hospitals, decentralized and dispersed over areas of ten square kilometers around their former centers. Nearly every student had volunteered for battle. Ho Ang Hoa, the national secretary of the Student Union, told us: "The problem now is not how to fight U.S. aggression, but how to fight U.S. aggression while improving our studies. Students must study as

well as fight if they are to triumph in all ways over imperialism."
Even with the bombings, there were twice as many students in the
country that year as the one before, and 98 percent of the seniors
graduated as compared to only 90 percent a year earlier. These
accomplishments can be appreciated only with an understanding
of the conditions of student life, which were hardly conducive to
studying. The pedagogical school had, for example, to disperse
fifteen times in the last six months because of bombings. Most
students were now organized into self-defense militia units and
practiced antiaircraft fighting between classes and after school.
Women, in many cases became superior marksmen to men, and
were commonly placed in charge of battalions and commanded
self-defense corps. Much of the nation's electricity had been destroyed, so students made gas lamps by which to study in the
trenches while keeping watch for raids. A couple of weeks before
we arrived, a class of agricultural students making studies of sea
plants in Tonkin Gulf were strafed and killed by U.S. planes.
Vietnam is a very long way from Sather Gate or Harvard Square.

The history of how we came to this point is enough to un-
hinge the sturdiest of minds. In what surely must be the most
outstanding American success story in the Horatio Alger tradition, Ngo Dinh Diem went from a Maryknoll Seminary in New
Jersey to Chief of State of the "Republic of South Vietnam." Contrary to the Geneva Convention which allowed no more than 685
military advisers from a single nation, the President dispatched
ten thousand "advisors" who, as one commentator remarked, were
"advising" their way through the jungles, often engaging the
enemy in hand-to-hand advice. Bobby Kennedy said at the time,
"The United States is in a war in Vietnam. American troops will
stay till we win." A resolve that, were the Attorney General to
have taken toward the citizens councils of Mississippi by dispatch-
ing an equal number of "advisors," would have rung his pro-
nouncements on democracy far less hollow.

While Uncle Ho was held in great affection and admiration throughout Vietnam, there was little of the cult often found in revolutionary situations. Fewer pictures of Ho could be seen in Hanoi than there are today of Nixon in Washington, D.C. We had the opportunity to see Ho on two occasions. The first came at the 20th anniversary celebration of the DRV independence. It was held in the evening inside the National Assembly Hall two nights before the National Day, to avoid possible disturbances from American planes. Included in the audience was the militia battalion responsible for downing the 500th U.S. plane. Fierce competition was held throughout the provinces for that honor. As the heat and humidity grew in the auditorium, Ho opened his shirt to his undershirt and removed his sandals. We were struck by the informality, but the Vietnamese took it as a matter of course, and we were reminded again of our arrival at the airport. The second time we saw the President was at the opera. Immediately before the first act, he slipped in the side door and took a seat at the rear of the first section. We would not have noticed his entrance at all, unobtrusive as it was, had not one of our companions spotted him.

Ho's informality and relationship to his people could be compared only to what I saw years later with Fidel and Cuba. One day, months before our visit to Hanoi, President Ho phoned the Youth Federation to say he was going to tour the provinces for the next couple of months, so please arrange for the Young Pioneers to take over the Presidential Palace and grounds. The Palace, formerly the home of the French colonial governor, and its grounds are as big and every bit as elegant as Washington's White House. (Ho preferred only to entertain at the Palace, living instead in an unassuming three-room bungalow elsewhere on the grounds.) For the next two months, 200,000 Young Pioneers camped on the grounds and had the run of the Palace itself.

When we were in the provinces, we found that children would warn villagers of an approaching air raid by running through the streets shouting, "John is coming, John is coming." We were told that Ho had begun this by deriving "John" from Johnson, adapting the name to the monosyllabic Vietnamese. We wondered aloud if they knew that in the American idiom, "John" means toilet. They smiled, telling us that Uncle Ho visited the United States many years ago as a seaman, and was no doubt familiar with American slang.

Of all of Ho's remarkable qualities as a revolutionary leader, a virtual Renaissance Man, perhaps most extraordinary was his ability to educate an entire population. As a result of 20 years of campaigning by Ho, the people of the DRV had an entirely different concept of war than we Americans. When the United States fights a war, it is against a whole population, no distinctions are made. But the Vietnamese fight against "imperialism" and the U.S. aggressors. Almost every Vietnamese we met, no matter how tragic their own personal losses had been, expressed to us friendship for the American people and high regard especially for the democratic movements in our country. We were told, for example, of a U.S. Air Force pilot, Dixon, who had been shot down, crashed into the sea, drowned and was washed ashore. The villagers who shot down his plane also recovered his body. He had been buried, flowers were planted on his grave, and the plot of ground was regularly cared for. The villagers have invited his parents to visit the grave when the war ends. To the Vietnamese, he was one more pawn in the U.S. Government's game. At the same time, Mrs. Alice Herz, the German refugee who had burned herself to death in Detroit to protest the war atrocities, was revered in Vietnam. A nationwide silent vigil was held for her on the receipt of news of her death, and a street in Hanoi is named for her.

Yet, while retaining their basic humanity and idealism in the face of 25 years of daily atrocities, the Vietnamese remained firm in their determination. They enjoyed telling us about the futility of U.S. planes dropping half a million propaganda leaflets on a province in an attempt at psychological warfare. The villagers gathered up the leaflets and brought them to a central place where they set a bonfire and held an anti-imperialist rally. UPI not long after reported that that the U.S. army was dropping aspirin on the NLF territories southeast of Saigon. "It was felt this would show the affluence of the United States—we could give them medicine their own leaders could not," Major Conrad Hausman cum Joseph Heller explained.

We asked to be allowed to go to "the front," the name given to the southern provinces of the DRV suffering from the most severe bombing. After a week in Hanoi, we left for Thanh Hoa, then undergoing daily raids. We had to make the trip by night, as the road leading south from the capital was bombed and strafed each day. Driving without lights, we continued on to Thanh Hoa as part of a military convoy, several hours long. We had been given to understand, through the U.S. press, that road travel had become impossible as bombs had destroyed the country's network of bridges. But we crossed several dozen on the way south; only three had been destroyed. In two cases we were forced to cross the rivers by ferry, and in the other a prefab bridge was up to keep traffic flowing at night and would be taken down before dawn, giving planes the impression the bridge was still destroyed. In the villages we entered, one heard a constant stream of singing, poetry reading and storytelling. Before we left Hanoi, we had met dozens of artists, poets, actresses and musicians who had come south to "the front" for months at a time to entertain and to participate in the self-defense corps. Everyone was armed, and presumably from this came the U.S. rationale of bombing homes and calling them military barracks.

Thanh Hoa itself was beautiful, its lushness in parts reminding one of Jack London's Valley of the Moon. The province contains the Ham Rong bridge, one of Robert McNamara's original "must" targets, and upon which day and night bombings rained down for four months prior to our visit. According to the Vietnamese, 58 planes had been downed in that period. The bridge itself didn't cost as much as two aircraft, and wasn't worth the cost of any of the human lives that McNamara had spent. We spoke to Ngo Thi Tuyen, a 19-year-old militia woman in the Nam Nan village in Thanh Hoa. On the first day of bombings directed at the Ham Rong bridge, the job of Sister Tuyen was to supply the militia on the other side of the half-mile long bridge. She is slight, weighing 98 pounds, quite average for a Vietnamese. Under the heavy attack of several dozen jet planes, Sister Tuyen carried 220 lbs. of ammunition on her back across the bridge. We asked her how she could manage this and she replied, "It had to be done." One older peasant explained: "If we do not win, then our children will, and if they do not, then our grandchildren will. We are prepared to fight for many years." But he added, "The question is not fighting for and winning a victory. Rather, if we do not fight, we will die, and we will lose our freedom and independence. The question then is not victory or defeat, but life or death."

At dawn on the morning of our arrival we visited the site of Hospital Number 71. Formerly a major tubercular sanatorium with a complex of 30 buildings, it was now a jumble of ruins. We were told that the 500-bed hospital was the victim of three separate raids, the last one with over 100 bombs. Nguyen Thuai, the director, took us about, showing us where 40 patients and five doctors had gone to their deaths. For a mile in any direction, the peasant villages surrounding the hospital were also leveled. We asked the director if it were possible that the hospital might have been mistaken from the air to be a military barracks. He replied that there were no barracks in that area, that the hospital had been there for five years, and that on top of each of its 30 buildings large red crosses had been painted. Medical workers believed that hospitals had become prime targets, objects of terror. They reported that several dozen had been destroyed throughout the country, all in situations similar to Number 71, all with red crosses on the roof-tops, all far distant from any military installations. The most famous was the Quynh Lap Leper Sanatorium on the seacoast. We were told that Quynh Lap had been subjected to fourteen separate raids, killing 120 patients, and that the last raid was aimed at the funeral of the previous dead and killed several mourners and destroyed the coffins.

Because of this pattern, medical workers had decentralized the provincial and district hospitals, dispersing sections of each into surrounding villages. We paid a visit to one of these village units and met with the patients. We saw a seven-year-old boy who had been playing in a rice paddy, when a plane spotted him, flew in and strafed him, blowing his legs off. We met a 28-year-old mother of two, who was working the fields when a plane strafed her. She was three months pregnant at the time but lost the baby, as her back was broken. Her legs will be permanently paralyzed. In no way could they have been mistaken for "military installations." A half-dozen other such victims lived in this small unit, all there was room for along with the normal hospital cases. Electricity for surgery had always been available in the regular hospitals, but these makeshift units had to make do with dry cell flashlight batteries.

We visited the Dai Thang agricultural co-op which had suffered through four raids and 50 deaths, mainly women and children, in the three weeks prior to our arrival. The co-op consisted of 170 households, or 800 persons. Under the French, the village peasants owned no land, had no education, no medicine and little food. Food output had now been almost doubled and the co-op had paved roads, schools and an animal husbandry complex. Illiteracy, which had been universal eleven years earlier, was now erased. Over 100 youths from the village were studying at universities. But progress would now come slower: the United States had "escalated" a war these people had not been fighting.

Two-thirds of the co-op's houses were now destroyed, some by napalm; many children were dead, some by Lazy Dog antipersonnel bombs. As we met with the peasants, we heard the planes approaching and we were herded through the village, across some paddies, to stand beside the trenches, prepared to enter the tunnels that lead away from the populated areas. These planes had a different destination, however, and we were in no danger. We repeated this experience four times that day. Others were not so fortunate. At the Nga Ba Moi Sanatorium, five elderly people were killed; in the Thieu Nguyen village nursery school, 25 children and three teachers died; 40 others perished at the raid on Kieu Eai village; the bombings of the Tu Tiu marketplace killed at least 29; and seven peasants were killed while working in the rice paddies. In the six months prior to our trip, there had been 2,100 such raids on Thanh Hoa province. Hundreds of factories, schools, hospitals, marketplaces, Buddhist pagodas, Catholic churches and fishing vessels had been destroyed. The United States had dropped rockets, napalm, phosphorous bombs, time bombs, Lazy Dogs, and even air-to-ground missiles, according to the peasants we met.

Thanh Hoa province had a population of 1.9 million people living primarily in large delta areas and along a long coast line. Since 1954, they have constructed a major textile factory, a food processing plant, sugar refineries, blast furnaces, and a fertilizer manufacturing complex. Five thousand youth brigadiers rebuilt the 90 kilometers of railway destroyed by the French before their final defeat. They have also built several dams and dikes to prevent crops from becoming water-logged. In the DRV, young people were the bulwark of socialism. We were told of Nguyen Ba Ngoc, a fourth grade student who, after a bombing raid on a nearby nursery school, herded two small children to shelter. When the raid ended, he went to get the other children and was hit by rockets. He dragged the other children to safety but died himself of burns and loss of blood. His story is repeated in the young lives of hundreds of others. We met fourteen-year-old Le Van Cung of Thap Linh village. Cung was studying in school the April past when the bombs hit. He and his classmates entered the village to put out the fire and save the smaller children. While he was carrying a small baby a plane swooped down to strafe the village and wounded Cung in both legs and one foot. Every day since, the doctors had had to remove splinters of bone. He explained to us that if the baby had lost his life, the country loses a human being. His loss is a loss for all. Cung smiled his sad smile and said he was pleased to meet his American uncles and asked us to give his regards to all his uncles and aunts in the United States. Another, Sister Dinh, a blast furnace laborer and militia woman, was napalmed while defending her factory, and is scarred all over her body. Her hair had fallen out (she was eighteen years old), she is without two fingers, and her ears bleed each day for long periods. But she reported that even while defending the country, her compatriots had increased production.

Sister Phuong Hanh worked as a waitress in a restaurant, served in the militia and sang the most tender lullabies I'd ever heard. We had many talks about the life of young people and, when one of us asked her what was the first thing she looked for in a man, she replied after some thought, "a fighting spirit for the fatherland." I asked her why she fought and what she thought the war was really about. She told me that for 1,100 years the Vietnamese have suffered through outside aggression and foreign domination, that throughout those years they struggled in wars of liberation and achieved a victory recognized throughout the world in 1954 with the Geneva Accords. Now a new aggressor had come and once again they must suffer atrocities to defend their homeland but once again they would be victorious. "You know," she said, "we are a poor country, but we are jealous of our independence and proud of our accomplishments. We work hard each day in the fields or in the factories, and when work is done we have poetry readings and storytelling and we get together and sing. And late at night under the stars we go with our sweethearts down to the river to have heart-to-heart talks. That is why we fight; to preserve our way of life." That evening we sat under a crescent moon together. The Vietnamese girls took our hands and we talked of many things, barely mentioning the war. They sang songs of love and Hieu remarked, "You see our girls are very militant, but when it comes to music they prefer romantic songs." Our circle was again interrupted by rockets and flares lighting up the sky as the planes returned. When the raid passed, we were told it was time to leave Thanh Hoa and a half hour later, glanced back to see more bombs and rockets. It was painful to know that some of these comrades to whom we'd come to feel so close would be blown apart or burned to death by the flying crematoria that serves as the United States Air Force.

Of course, one thing that immediately strikes a North American abroad is how enormously rich his country is. The Soviet Union, pictured in our media as "just like us" in 1965 produced less than a quarter-million autos and it is the rare Soviet young couple that can afford to live apart from parents. In London, Rome and Paris refrigerators are more than a bit scarce. But when one arrives in Hanoi or Peking or Havana, there remain no grounds for comparison. A sense of Vietnam can be gotten from Party First Secretary Le Duan stating a few years ago, "There will be no harm if we temporarily abstain from eating sweets made of groundnuts and export them instead to pay for machines." Nearly any single store in New York contains more of what is conveniently called "goods" than any square block in Vietnam or Cuba. One of the villains in Truffaut's *Shoot the Piano Player* lists the things he owns—a "British hat of Australian wool, a musical cigarette lighter, a Snorkel pen from America"; he complains: "I'm so stuffed with possessions I could puke."

My thoughts precisely when, back in Hanoi, we had an opportunity to interview USAF Captain Robert Daughtrey of Eagle Pass, Texas, one of the captured pilots. Captain Daughtrey had flown from Korat Air Force Base in Thailand, his target being the Ham Rong bridge in Thanh Hoa. When his plane was hit by anti-aircraft fire, he lost altitude rapidly and ejected only 300 feet above ground, breaking both arms in his fall. When we met him a month later both arms were still in casts and he was totally *far-blondjet*. Reluctant to talk in the beginning, he perked up upon learning we were recently in the States and he asked us about the baseball standings. After we had exhausted the National League, we snuck in a question about his capture and subsequent treatment. Daughtrey said that after his fall he was in great pain and entertained the thought that his captors might kill him. He discounted the possibility of torture although he said he had read *Life* accounts of Americans torturing Vietnamese and assumed the reverse was most likely true as well. The villagers who shot him had also found him in pain and, after disarming him, offered him a thermos of hot tea and a loaf of bread. They then dressed his wounds and turned him over to the local hospital. He was now kept in a hospital near Hanoi in a room with another American prisoner so that he had company. He seemed grateful for the way he had been treated and told us he had had three operations on one arm already and seemed confident of its full recovery. We asked Daughtrey if, after returning to base following his sorties, the pilots talked among themselves about the war. He told us that the war itself was never a subject for discussion, that the purposes of the war are not considered, and that to think about the war might in fact lead to a breakdown in military discipline. We are soldiers, he said, and that is like being parts of a machine. (Enter Mario Savio, on cue.) Machines don't think, continued Daughtrey. I pointed out to him that human beings do think, however, that soldiers are presumably human beings as well, and that in fact his army was losing to an army which both thought deeply about why it fought *and* still maintained its military discipline. Such talk fazed Daughtrey not at all.

He asked us if the Ham Rong bridge, his target, was still standing and when we replied it still stood in servicable condition, he smiled. It was like a sporting contest, he explained. I asked him why he joined the Air Force and he replied that it was a "good job," with retirement benefits, PX privileges and good pay; he was not making enough money on the farm in Texas. This was just a good job. I asked why he didn't get another job. He said he loves to fly. I asked why didn't he fly commercially. He said, no, man, that's just like driving a bus; he liked to just get up there by himself and zoom and roll over. I asked if he considered the fact that in his zooming he was killing people and destroying their country. He replied that he never thought they would shoot back. As the meeting drew to a close, we told Daughtrey that we would be returning to the U.S. soon and asked him if he would like us to bring a message to his wife, children or father in Del Rio, Texas. He had no message for his wife or children but asked us to have his father return the two air conditioners to the store for him as he "won't be needing them now." This was about the moxie of this poor vinyl-minded young American for freedom. He was a nice fellow, kept a good sense of humor and was a typical product of his system. He couldn't believe his government could do wrong and had no real understanding of the seriousness of what he had done or the spot he was in. He had no real sense of social responsibility and absolutely no political interest, let alone awareness. He is the stuff of which Jaycees across our country are made of; he is loyal to his family, generous with his friends. He just wants to live the good life of air conditioners and PX privileges. And he would napalm a civilian population in Vietnam without thinking once.

When we were in Thanh Hoa, we examined the contents of

one downed pilot's survival kit. There was the customary compass, maps, rations and cooking utensils. And there was the poison capsule to be swallowed, presumably in order to escape torture. I wonder now how many, if any, American flyboys have died at the hands of DuPont Chemical and the USAF in order to avoid a punishment they would never have received. Also in the kit we found a U. S. Armed Forces phrasebook of what to say upon capture. Written in several languages by the Office of Naval Intelligence, the book was called *Pointee-Talkee*. The *no-tickee-no-washee* racism came all the way from the top of the Great Society. Phrases every captured pilot should know, included in this bombadier's *Berlitz*, were: "Will you accept gold?"; "Where is the nearest telephone?"; and "Can you direct me to the nearest friendly guerrillas?", a question, I. F. Stone pointed out, the Pentagon has been asking wistfully about North Vietnam for several years.

One other item of interest in the kit was an American flag, accompanied by a phrase written in English, Burmese, Thai, Laotian, Cambodian, Chinese, French, Dutch, Malaysian, Indonesian and Vietnamese. An item that bodes none too well for lands speaking those tongues, it seems to me. The phrase read as follows: "I am a citizen of the United States of America. I do not speak your language. Misfortune forces me [he's just been shot out of the sky by these same people, remember] to seek your assistance in obtaining food, shelter and protection. Please take me to someone who will provide for my safety and see that I am returned to my people. My government will reward you." Now, Sister Hanh in Thanh Hoa is different, of course, from many Vietnamese but her thoughts about the war were typical of the people we met; at the same time, while not all soldiers are Captain Daughtreys, his particular mentality generally approximates that of the U.S. military. Symbolically, in my mind, the war had become one between a poor people fighting for their right to life, to be able to have heart-to-heart talks with their sweethearts at night, and, on the other hand, the richest nation in history, wishing to impose on these people its great society of air conditioners and *pointee-talkee*. Lyndon himself was to remark a year later at a U.S. base in South Korea that the reason for these wars is that "There are three billion of them and only 200 million of us; they want what we have, but we ain't gonna give it to them."

eleven

Plei Do Lim, South Vietnam—Many American soldiers sent to South Vietnam as military advisers have found their greatest satisfaction in setting up a kind of peace corps in the villages. "Every time we have to kill," one West Point graduate said, "It's a failure for us. It means we haven't been able to get across to the people in the area."

—UPI

By every reliable index, America will be living with its new style of normalcy for some time to come. . . . In Los Angeles, for example, the cops are experimenting with a 20-ton armored personnel carrier that can tote twenty fully-equipped men and boasts a .30 caliber machine gun, tear-gas launchers, a smoke screen device, chemical fire extinguishers, hoses, and a siren so high-powered that its wail can temporarily stun rioters. "When I look at this thing," says one L.A. police planner, "I think, My God, I hope we never have to use it. But we might as well be prepared."

—NEWSWEEK.

The trip back from Hanoi was miserable. It didn't matter any more what the U.S. Government might do to us. After all, a couple of us had volunteered to stay and fight if the Vietnamese thought it would be of use. Rather our dilemma was how to be of use back in the States. Sitting around our hotel in Peking one night we plunged to new depths of misery. Chris, the newsman, told of a movie premiere for Andy Warhol's *Blow Job* he had attended before leaving New York. How could he tell those people about Thanh Hoa; what would it mean to them. A friend we remembered, a long-time radical who had been black listed, recently fired from Chris's radio station to appease Senate investigators, was now working in Los Angeles. Committed as he was, he would take no job under $10,000 a year, and was now doing promotion work for a firm producing *soleless sandals*. How does one explain that to a young Vietnamese under treatment after two full years of torture. We were on our way back to our country in which, *The London Evening Standard* told us en flight, "Bobby Baker, who commutes between his huge vending machine interests in California and his wife in Washington, has evidently decided to make the most of his fame while it lasts. His Carousel Motel, out in the uniquely hideous Maryland resort of Ocean City, is no longer its old anonymous self. Baker's name has been emblazoned on the hoardings, printed on the advertisements and embroidered on the table-cloths and napkins, which diners who know history when they see it are stuffing into their pockets as souvenirs."

In Moscow, we learned that Laurence Olivier's *Othello* had the night before received fifteen minutes of bravos, led by Premier Kosygin, his wife, and their guests, the representatives of the DRV and the NLF and their wives. To counter the command performance, the *Standard* reported, the U. S. Embassy had offered for the diplomatic corps a screening of Ian Fleming's *From Russia With Love*. That was the same week that Wayne Morse revealed to the Senate, CIA and Pentagon contingency plans for the overthrow of at least 40 separate governments; under the guise of social science research *à la* the Camelot project in Chile, potential targets included Ethiopia, Japan, Ghana, Nigeria, Sudan, Guinea, Brazil, Cyprus, Liberia, Egypt, Indonesia, Korea, Panama, Cuba, Germany, and Venezuela. Since then of course Ghana, Brazil, Indonesia and Panama have had *coups d'état,* Indonesia's resulting in the slaughter of as many as 800,000 "Communists or suspected Communists." And back in Minneapolis that week, Byron B. Gentry, commander in chief of the Veterans of Foreign Wars, like a comic strip character with balloons above his head for thoughts, declared that America's "addiction to peace" posed one of the gravest threats to the nation's security. What could we, with that particular monkey on our backs, tell the good folks of Minneapolis about Vietnam? Home in San Francisco, I learned that the FBI had been around to my friends every several days to tell me, it turns out, that they had infiltrated the Minute Men and that that nasty little *mishpocheh* had listed me number two on their top ten "kill list." Paul Krassner of *The Realist* suggested I wear an Avis button. How were we to break through the hermetic seals by which the best souls of our country were being protected.

At our press conference at the Overseas Press Club in New York, all the press came to hear the first of their countrymen to visit the country with which we were at war, a story which merited the attention of the corps of newsmen present. The next day, we received minor mention in the back pages of *The Times* and *The Post-Dispatch* of St. Louis; no other media, outside the left, paid any attention, establishing again that old rule of thumb that no news is indeed no news. I decided to go on a speaking tour and my next six months were occupied by three and four appearances daily, at churches, universities, union halls, living rooms, from Hawaii to Boston, Baltimore to Vancouver, to audiences ranging from 10,000 to seven, telling of our trip.

A debate was raging in the ranks of the movement over what was the primary demand to make on the Government—withdrawal from Vietnam, or negotiations with the Vietnamese. While slogans did not concern me, I believe the line of reasoning that demanded withdrawal was essential, and I argued for that line wherever I went, a position that put me in trouble with many good friends, as well as most not-so-good friends. I appreciated the concern of those who demanded negotiations first; they wished most of all to stop the fighting and killings and to bring peace to Vietnam. But 1,100 years of people's wars against foreign domination had taught the Vietnamese that peace without freedom is not peace, and that is what the Vietnamese taught us. There could be no peace in that land except a peace free of foreign domination, including troops. Friends would argue that sure, we should get out but we had to show people a reasonable way to get out. Summoning up all the logic my old favorite Mark Twain might bring to bear on the question, I figured that first of all people were not shown a reasonable way to go in. And that we could get out the same way as we went in: by plane and by boat. The way to stop bombings and torture was to simply stop bombings and torture.

A major motivation for those who demanded negotiations was a wish to stop the bloodshed immediately, fearing that American military might could abolish Vietnam. We are too powerful, the argument went; we are not France. This big-nation chauvinism, while motivated by humanism, seemed to me chauvinism nevertheless and did not take into account all of the facts of the war. To say the United States was too powerful an enemy was to do precisely what the Pentagon wished, *i.e.* to abandon each national liberation struggle. McNamara and Maxwell Taylor were telling the world that Vietnam was where the U.S. was making its stand. We will show you, they said, that the United States is too powerful an adversary. They were serving notice on the peoples of Latin America and Africa that they too faced B-52 raids, napalm and Marine invasions if they engaged in wars of national liberation. The Vietnam war was and remains the major struggle in the world of anti-imperialist forces against the major imperialist power. McNamara and Taylor grasped correctly the significance of the war, I argued, and the antiwar movement would be wrong to do otherwise.

The Vietnamese themselves granted that the U.S. would give up the war not only because of continued military defeats but also because it was becoming increasingly isolated by world opinion, and because the U.S. public would tire of the war as they did of Korea. Of course, we were not the French, but the French did control Hanoi and Haiphong, and the transportation and communications networks of all of Vietnam. They had twice the amount of troops we had in 1965, and all were professionals. The socialist world was much more powerful now than it had been before 1954. Much more of Africa and Asia was politically independent of the West than was the case prior to Dien Bien Phu. Cambodia was now independent and increasingly hostile to the United States; the Vietnamese controlled Vietnam north of the seventeenth parallel; the Pathet Lao controlled much of Laos. If the U.S. were to commit troops to those areas, it would be committing those troops to suicide. The NLF continued to control 80 percent of South Vietnam, the U.S. had not gained back one inch of ground, even with the B-52's and the Marines. At home in the States, the war was not popular. People were becoming increasingly concerned and confused, if not yet hostile. Most of Johnson's popular support came not from a desire to keep fighting, but because of a confused patriotic belief that the President knows best, that he has the facts. There were good reasons for the concern and confusion: people still remembered the atrocities of Hitler and it was difficult to accept our government doing the same thing for "freedom"; the constant change of regimes in Saigon, none of which were elected, made a bad case for the argument that the U.S. was there at the request of the "democratic government of South Vietnam"; it was difficult to explain 200,000 troops napalming and raping a country for "freedom," when the Attorney General couldn't provide 100 voter registrars in Alabama; people voted for "Johnson" and got "Goldwater."

A major source of the chauvinism infecting the movement here was to be found in the "brave little warrior" way of viewing the NLF, a modern corollary to the "nobel savage" concept. All too often it was suggested that we should understand the deep feelings of the Vietnamese but they really didn't know what was best. The DRV, the argument went, might well have fine generals but nothing they said about the course of the war could be compared in validity to the average peacenik Yank, who, after all, lives in the belly of the beast itself and therefore best knows this country's power. Yet, peculiarly, when Germany was bombarding Great Britain, and before that Spain, when it was invading Russia, no one suggested those countries negotiate with Hitler. Jean-Paul Sartre wrote before the end of the Algerian war:

The "liberals" are stupefied, they admit that we were not polite enough to the natives, that it would have been wiser and fairer to allow them certain rights insofar as it was possible; they ask nothing better than to admit them in batches and without sponsors to that very exclusive club, our species; and now this barbarous, mad outburst doesn't spare them any more than the bad settlers. The Left at home is embarrassed; they know the true situation of the natives, the merciless oppression they are subjected to; they do not condemn their revolt, knowing full well that we have done everything to provoke it. But all the same, they think to themselves, there are limits; these guerrillas should be bent on showing that they are chivalrous, that would be the best way of showing they are men. Sometimes the Left scolds them—"You're going too far; we won't support you any more." The natives don't give a damn about their support; for all the good it does them they might as well stuff it up their backsides. Once their war began, they saw this hard truth; that every single one of us had made his bit, has got something out of them; they don't need to call anyone to witness; they'll grant favored treatment to no one.

There is one duty to be done, one end to achieve; to thrust out colonialism by every means in their power. The more far seeing among us will be, in the last resort, ready to admit this duty and this end; but we cannot help seeing in this ordeal by force the altogether inhuman means that these less-than-men make of us to win the concession of a charter of humanity. Accord it to them at once, then, and let them endeavor by peaceful undertaking to deserve it. Our worthiest souls contain racial prejudice.

Traveling the country again was exhilarating at first, exhausting after a week or two. Fringe benefits helped, like being invited by the Honolulu Junior Chamber of Commerce to address audiences in the islands for a week or two. One day I received a call from some friends in Toronto, saying there was to be an International Teach-In at the University, attended by 9,000 and would I come and represent the North Vietnamese. I said that was of course impossible, I was not Vietnamese, I had no credentials from the DRV, they should invite the Vietnamese directly, and if it was impossible for them to come I would come and explain what I understood to be the DRV position, after having talked to leaders of that country. As it turned out I did go to Toronto and was to be on a panel, with the U.N. delegate from Cambodia, and Professor Robert Scalapino of the University of California and a State Department consultant. Upon arriving in Toronto, I was told that Scalapino refused to appear on the platform with me and would I please drop out. I suggested Scalapino leave; I was placing no obstacles to his speaking. The Teach-In committee bowed to Scalapino and I was removed from the program. Local peace and student movement activists learned of what had happened and started a sit-in at the stadium. Speakers on other panels referred to the affair. The Teach-In, broadcast in its entirety over national

Canadian television, came under fire for removing me, in editorials across the country. When the Vietnam panel actually started, some students began throwing chairs. Shouts of "Chicken Scalapino" filled the stadium. The movement announced that an auditorium had been secured for me to speak that evening at a counter-teach-in. With Guyanese leader Cheddi Jagan on the dais, and the auditorium overflowing so that an outdoor public address system had to be set up, I spoke about the trip. That was even more fun than the Hawaiian Jaycees.

Everywhere I went, local papers covering my appearance noted that the State Department was considering removing my passport for breaking its restrictions. *Life* magazine and Bay Area right-wingers made much of the fact that I now sported a ring made from scraps of a downed U.S. aircraft, and AP reported I was being considered for possible prosecution for "trading with the enemy." I argued that I had traded nothing, the ring was a gift, and in any case it was made in the USA, not Vietnam. Nothing further happened, although several months later, after Staughton Lynd, Herbert Aptheker and Tom Hayden visited Hanoi, my passport was lifted, not to be returned until the Supreme Court ruled favorably three years later. Rings similar to mine have now become plentiful in the movement as a result of the many exchanges with the Vietnamese held since then. Just before Christmas that year, 1965, Lyndon Johnson, in announcing his new "peace offensive," said he was willing to go anywhere and see anyone in his search for peace in Vietnam. In the President's words, he would "knock on any door." Immediately a dozen diplomats of the caliber of Averell Harriman and Arthur Goldberg were dispatched to the Vatican, Ottawa, Delhi, Paris, Warsaw and other world capitals. But the Pope, Lester Pearson, Charles de Gaulle, Gomulka and the rest were not fighting in Vietnam. The two doors on which LBJ never knocked were those belonging to the NLF and the DRV. In that season of celebration of the Prince of Peace, it was left to Lynd, Aptheker and Hayden to go where angels and the President of the United States feared to tread. Their path has been followed many times since, each one another crack in the Paper Curtain our government has erected.

That winter I was asked to become campaign manager for the Robert Scheer congressional campaign in Oakland and Berkeley, the most important and most exciting radical candidacy since the days of New York's Vito Marcantonio. But I felt spent. Besides going to school and working, I had been for practical purposes a full-time political worker for seven years. The only way to get out from under the load was to leave the Bay Area. This, combined with other personal reasons, helped me leave California. One obviously did not escape the war of course. The crisis of U.S. capitalism, unable to meet the needs of its people, was exacerbated immensely in every way by Vietnam. The Republic had become ever more polarized over the questions of black liberation and racist oppression. The pathological fear that arose among whites at the specter of black power became clear to me in an NYU adult education class in The Literature of Social Protest. The class was assigned to read, among other works, books by Baldwin, Malcolm and Fanon. Most of the students, all white, were frightened by what they read. None would admit to racist thoughts, all of them had among their best friends, etc., all deeply believed that for all its problems this was the most just of societies. But when pushed as to why they feared the call for black power, one woman spoke for the class when she said that if blacks got their rightful share of power they might seek revenge. In the darkest reaches of her soul, she feared that blacks might do unto whites what had been done unto them these last four centuries. When push came to shove, she understood profoundly, despite protestations to the contrary, her own racist nature. Otherwise, why fear revenge. A couple of years back, the Boston, Massachusetts, School Board attempted unique solution to the problem when, in an attempt to remove schools in the Chinese ghetto from the category of "racially imbalanced," it declared the Chinese to be white.

The madness inherent to the system now approaches hysteria with the crisis. The cries of law and order curdle the blood. In Bryn Athyn, Pennsylvania, Lacklan Pitcairn, millionaire treasurer of the Pitcairn Company, announced, "We have to live within the law," as he turned his daughter in to the police for possession of marijuana. Mrs. Pitcairn supported her husband's move. "It was the only thing to do," she said. On one day last winter, January 22, 1969, in Da Nang, South Vietnam, a 20-year-old U.S. Marine was found not guilty of premeditated murder in the deaths of four Vietnamese civilians, at least one of whom died at the hands of an impromptu Marine firing squad out on an ambush patrol, another of whom was hanged by the patrol. Ten thousand miles away and half a day earlier, in Jacksonville, Florida, a white man who admitted firing a rifle at a black youth was found not guilty of murder. The sniper, cruising through the Jacksonville ghetto after the assassination of Martin Luther King, killed the eighteen-year-old with a single bullet between the eyes, as he sat on his bicycle sipping a soda with friends. The victim was home on leave from the Air Force.

Psychology professor Bruno Bettelheim of the University of Chicago, following the traditions of that school which fielded Leopold and Loeb and the atomic bomb, believes there is no crisis in the country save perhaps in the field of child psychology. In the burlesque of old, the off-center toupee and slipping on the banana peel, oft-repeated as it might have been, was always a hard act to follow. Similarly, Dr. Bettelheim had to testify before the House Special Subcommittee on Education, following on the heels of San Francisco State's own beloved S. I. Hayakawa. But Bettelheim rose to the occasion and can now be considered Top Banana of American education. Telling Congress that some student protesters had not matured emotionally beyond the temper tantrum level, he argued they were guilt-ridden as a result of their exemption from military service. The good doctor testified under oath that the old college rituals—the fraternity house and football rally—had declined, leading students to look to "the sit-ins and rebellion" for excitement and a spirit of comradeship. Further, that many young people were critical of their parents for a lack of strength and conviction and looked outside their families for father figures to admire. "This is the reason," he said, "why so many of our radicals embrace Maoism, why they chant in their demonstrations 'Ho Ho Ho Chi Minh,' exactly as another generation of students chanted at their football rallies. These are strong fathers with strong convictions who powerfully coerce their children to follow their commands."

Another congressional hearing, this by a House Judiciary subcommittee, heard an equally fascinating battery of witnesses as it considered legislation to make desecration of the flag a federal crime. Worked up over recent Vietnam protests, Representative James H. Quillen of Tennessee testified that "I really believe there couldn't be any penalty too strict short of the firing squad." Congressman Maston O'Neal of Georgia said that "oral abuse" of the national symbol should be classified as sedition. Asked to explain this novel concept, presumably because the Stars and Stripes had not previously been recorded as arousing prurient interest, the congressman explained that he was talking about people who "curse the flag." Another precinct was heard from when Pennsylvania Supreme Court Justice Michael A. Musmanno argued that Congress should provide that desecration cases be given priority, "because, if the conviction does not come until a year or two after the flag has been destroyed and the community outraged, the judge may be persuaded into misguided leniency, merely because of the intervention of time." The judge might consider auditioning for Western movies as the man who cries "Why wait for the law. Let's string 'em up now!" Desecration of the "enemy" flag warranted no such concern from Congress. Only a month before these hearings, UPI reported that a group of enterprising soldiers, members of the elite Green Berets, were doing a land office business in Saigon, selling bloodstained "Vietcong battle flags" to U.S. airmen, at $25 apiece. The Special Forces men, it seems, hired an old woman in a Saigon back street to sew a bundle of new "Vietcong flags." Then, in their contribution to the Great Ideas of Western Man, they stomped on the banners in the mud and sprinkled them with chicken blood. And what could be more obscene than Hubert Horatio Humphrey, that high school yearbook on wheels, being nominated for the Presidency over flailing police clubs, not having won even one primary in his own party's elections?

twelve

*I respect kindness to human beings first of all,
and kindness to animals. I don't respect the
law; I have a total irreverence for anything
connected with society except that which makes
the roads safer, the beer stronger, and the
food cheaper, and old men and old women warmer
in the winter and happier in the summer.*
                              —BRENDAN BEHAN

Be realists, demand the impossible!
                              —GRAFFITI

So now we have put a man on the moon. And of course it's a stupendous technological achievement. But it is one for others to marvel at. For myself it matters little. Perhaps because of a cultural lag, the moon shot is beyond me; I never did tune in too well to whatever national mania was current. One of the remarkable aspects of the United States and our vastness is the incredible gaps in cultures. I remember many years ago going to the De Young Museum in San Francisco's Golden Gate Park. A group of 30 or so black kids, about eight or nine years old, was being herded through the immaculate museum with patented descriptions of what they were seeing being reamed down their throats by their elderly teacher. When the group had boarded the bus for the trip back to school, museum guides discovered a couple of paintings had been slashed with penknives. The guides were of course abashed; we, however, viewed it as a cultural exchange. Maybe that's why I'm so unable to visualize a surrogate me up there in Apollo 11.

Or perhaps it's because, for the past dozen years, I've had lurking somewhere deep in my cranium a bit of a premonition that the other side of the moon would see the light faster than I would see the other side of 30 years. I'm not sure what the basis for this premonition is but I have had a number of very close friends die, even when I was a child. Someone once said that great men die early, whether at 25 or 85, and I know that this is true for good friends. These deaths and the premonition also probably help explain why in the last couple of years I've come to love children—not children in general but ones who are very special to me—and flowers, and all those things I was taught to love and which I rejected until these last few years, as I reach for 30. Whatever the case, these children, even in extended and repeated doses, excite me where Neil Armstrong moves me not in the least.

I should state, I suppose, that these lines are being written not with distance for retrospect, but less than 24 hours after Armstrong first touched down on the lunar surface, at the apex of the hysteria down here among fellow North American earthlings. A number of papers and magazines in their pre-blast-off special numbers, described the origins of the moon shot; how under President Kennedy, especially after the Playa Giron debacle, all stops were pulled out; how up through Johnson to Nixon, the goal was not to put a man on the moon, but to put an *American* man on the moon; how the nation, that is to say, U.S. imperialism, needed such a grand prestige victory to recoup its losses these last years. One needn't give it much thought to know with full certainty that the next years will see U.S. Information Agency offices around the world explaining that even though we cremate babies alive in Southeast Asia, even though we murdered Che Guevara, even though we are prepared to use tanks against Harlem and against Texas Southern University, even so, God dammit, we've got to be great, we put a man on the moon. And if the USIA will use it abroad, one already knows how it has been used at home—to create a newer, deeper, chauvinism over Our Way of Life.

Because Kennedy, Johnson and Nixon won. That was not a man on the moon, it was indeed an American man on the moon. And what name could possibly be more American than the All-American name itself, Armstrong. Eric Sevareid and other sophists made clear note of the fact that the first man on the moon would be more typically American than a Rockwell SatEvePost cover. He would be from a small Midwest town, blond, moon-faced, with a shy shucks, ma'm, grin. Now of course that's typical American for greetings cards and situation comedies. But who can argue that more typical might not be buck-shod Pat Boone, who merited father-of-the-year kudos a couple of years back for declaring that he'd rather see his own children shot before his "very eyes" than have them grow up under atheistic Communism. Another nomination I'd make for mosttypicalAmerican might be

Hans V. Tofte, CIA expert in clandestine operations, who a couple of years ago reported that two other CIA operatives visited his house, lifting from him not only the secret documents they were assigned by the agency to steal, but also $19,000 in jewels. Or, why not little sixteen-year-old Tommy Robinson of Brownsville, Texas, who shot up a jetliner loaded with 91 persons in an apparent hijack attempt to fly people to Cuba to show them "the evils of Communism," according to UPI. Said Tommy's mother: "He has always been extremely patriotic. He deplored draft card burners. He seemed to have some idea of taking some of these people who don't understand Communism to Cuba to prove to them that Communism just doesn't work." And what more typical American could be found than any one of the 5,000 stockbrokers, bankers and stock exchange clerks who mobbed the windows of the Stock Exchange, the steps of the Subtreasury, the rooftops and light poles surrounding the Morgan Guaranty Trust Company, crushing the roofs of parked cars and breaking the windows of banks in the nation's financial center in downtown Manhattan, all to catch a glimpse in the spring of 1969 of 21-year-old Francine Gottfied, 43–25–37. And who is more all-American than Chicago vice-squad officer Marvin Mandel who, stooping to his own level, entrapped, for an offer of a hundred bucks, Miss Neen Welch, campaign worker and self-proclaimed betrothed of Alabama's George Wallace. (Miss Welch may well have been researching a book on "the making of the presidential candidate, 1968.") Or, who could better take that small step of man, that one giant leap for mankind than Lyndon Johnson, the Mantovani of politics himself, who set up the 1968 Democratic National Convention in the city of his choice but who would not even venture into his own mass birthday party, considering it much too dangerous. And, as long as the P.R. department of NASA wanted the first man on the moon to hail from Sinclair Lewis's America, why not the maternal grandfather of eight-year-old Mark Wendell Painter in Gilbert, Iowa, who was rewarded the child by the Iowa Supreme Court because he would provide a "stable, dependable, conventional, middle-class, Middle-West background," as opposed to the boy's father, whom the court rejected as "unconventional, arty, Bohemian and probably intellectually stimulating"; the grandfather was found to be a "father figure of excellent reputation who regularly teaches a Sunday school class," the father to be "either an agnostic or an atheist" and "a political liberal"; in his father's home, the court said, "Mark would have more freedom of conduct and thought, with an opportunity to develop his individual talents. It would be more exciting and challenging in many respects, but romantic, impractical and unstable"; as evidence of the father's "bohemian-ism," the court asserted that "his main ambition is to be a free-lance writer and photographer."

What possibly is more "typically American" than the ads for "Forbes: Capitalist Tool", the businessman's magazine with 425,-000 subscribers; such as the one occuping a full page in *The Times* featuring a large photo of an East Indian, lying down, ema-ciated from starvation, ribs protruding, and asking: "Hey mister. Want to buy a shiny new car with white walls, air-conditioning, full power and stereo? Are you one of those people who thinks foreign countries should get off the dole and pay for what we send them? India did that. We are now holding the equivalent of two-thirds of the entire currency of India. They have paid it to us for food. And they are still starving. As a matter of fact, two billion of the world's people are near starvation. They are a very poor mar-ket for the things American business would like to sell them. Cars, for instance. Our government is up nights dealing with the world hunger problem. As Forbes says, 'In so doing, it will also create tremendous opportunities for businesses that have the knowhow, the foresight and the capital to help end hunger.' . . . Making good markets out of starving nations is such a huge opportunity for American business, Forbes recently did a special report called

'Feeding the world's hungry millions: How it will mean billions for U.S. Business.' "

Who might better represent U.S. interests in lunarland than the Pentagon official who has been directing joint U.S.-Spanish troop maneuvers in the Pyrenees to practice putting down any future rebellion against the fascist Franco regime. Or any of the men responsible for placing nerve gas on Okinawa, the discovery of which came at the exact time the Apollo 11 module touched down on the lunar surface. Is this any way to run a rocket program? You bet it is!

Someone once remarked that common sense is the insight that tells us that the world is flat. And it is that sense that leads the more ambitious and more optimistic of us to declare that in these days of moon landings, given all the unrest in the nation and the seeming inability of the system to cope with it, that we are in a revolutionary situation. But a more careful glance will tell us that if this is a revolutionary period for us, the ships will be falling off the seas' horizons any moment now. Power today is held by the class which owns the productive plant of the nation and the wealth flowing from it. The class in our society that is engaged in a constant quarrel with ownership over its share of this wealth is the working class, those whose means of livelihood depend entirely on the sale of their work-ability, whether physical or mental. This is the only class with the numbers, organizational ability, strategic location and the potential cohesion and discipline with which to wield a comparable counter-power. As one of the leaders of the Cuban revolution told me, the task of the vanguard in any industrial country is to give left leadership to the working class. And, while the movement has no greater need today, we have no vanguard. One does not become a vanguard by self-proclamation or claims of holding the franchise, but rather by earning that title.

When I first came to Berkeley eleven years ago, Daniel Bell declared that American capitalism had resolved its contradictions and that ideology was now dead. All my teachers argued that Marxism was a throwback to the days of the long-gone breadlines and Group Theater; the war had ended all that. When C. Wright Mills wrote his *Letter to The New Left,* he agreed that the ersatz prosperity we now lived in had indeed co-opted working people, that only students and intellectuals could serve as a new progressive force. And students have in fact been the advance agent in raising questions of the war economy, aggressive wars abroad, racist oppression, the need for a new order. This led to much early agreement with the academic consensus that workers were now part of the system, thus the need to turn to "the poor," the one possibly unco-opted group save the students themselves. From counter-communities to resistance, concepts dominated the movement which based themselves on the concept that while virtuous we could not be powerful; what was possible was only the building of oases of good in the desert of evil, to build Communism in a handful of communities. One was reminded of the anarchist Bakunin, who took power in one French town, declared the state dissolved, and was invaded and defeated shortly thereafter by troops of the regime.

What increasing numbers have now come to is the need to contend for, and indeed to win, power: that is revolution. And the only force that can contend for power with those who run this nation is an organized conscious working class. If the class is the force, it is the party that gives the class its leadership, its revolutionary will. And we must admit that, combined with the new economic situation in our country, McCarthyism did succeed in crippling and isolating revolutionary leadership of the workers. Those who are older, who fought the good fight against Fascism, both abroad and at home, who combated racism many years before it became copy for *Life,* who suffered the wrath of the most powerful imperialism in history, those who have done this and remain in the movement today deserve to be honored. Nevertheless they have much to learn from the young. The new militance should inspire many to shed their understandable, but still crippling, "gun-shyness." It will teach those who are willing to learn, a new sense of outrage, creative and bold techniques of struggle, a healthy skepticism of sacred cows, a constant questioning and reexamination of "proven concepts," and a renewed commitment to real democracy and constant vigilance against bureaucracy. The coming together of the most dedicated and advanced of the young with the old could provide us with the vanguard that we now lack.

It goes without saying that young radicals have much to learn from the past; but, in fact, they are learning. Our most recent past has too often seen many of us as laissez faire organizers promoting confrontations. Instead of concentrating on issues where victories could be won, the opposite sort of issue was deemed more desirable since it would guarantee the confrontation situations within which it would be possible to radicalize people. The situation itself, went the assumption, would be the major radicalizing element. But this approach presented a problem: people could have two reactions to becoming aware of the obstacles confronting us—they could become more radical and militant, but they could also conclude it is futile to struggle. The strategic problem we face, living now in a nonrevolutionary period, is how to build a revolutionary movement; how to fight for and win needed reforms in a revolutionary, not a reformist, manner.

The self-conception of the organizer has changed these last years. Initially there was a problem with the messianic approach —a rigid separation of the organizer from those to be organized. The organizers did not share the grievances of the people they worked with, they just empathized with them. Often the rhetoric about letting the people decide disguised a paternalism and really meant let the people think they were deciding, while the operative decisions were made either by default or at small closed meetings by the organizers. The role of organizer when seen in mechanical terms made for the absence of any clear concept of political leadership. Leadership tended to be equated with domination and manipulation, which led to a reliance on spontaneity, and in turn lead to frustations which stimulated manipulative tendencies. The process of organizing and fighting for an immediate demand creates an expanded potential to enlarge the understanding of the participants as to the meaning of the demand, the nature of the opposition, and the general social context in which the struggle is made. But this potential does not realize itself automatically or by fiat. The concrete outcome of a particular struggle will create both illusions about reform and, simultaneously, exaggerated despair and frustration. A conscious agency is necessary to clarify what was won and what remains to be won, why the society works as it does, and what must be done to change it. That is the role of the revolutionary, of what has traditionally been called the vanguard. In the United States today a vanguard is especially needed because, in addition to grievances of the level of consumption, there are those relating to the issues of freedom and power. Those that run this country have infinitely more flexibility to grant concessions on the former than the latter, and a vanguard, if you will, is necessary to cut through the illusions that flow from such concessions, to exercise revolutionary leadership in the course of reform struggles. That, not martyrdom, self-abnegation, nor charisma, is the essence of leadership. Manipulation is the consequence of trying to get people's assent but not their understanding; it results from placing undue emphasis on what people "get" from a situation—either a "victory" or a "confrontation"—and thus maneuvering them into that situation. But in fact a "victory" without understanding only creates illusions, and a defeat or abortive confrontation without understanding creates despair and cynicism.

A half-dozen years ago, Lenny Bruce used to do a routine about some peace movement leaders visiting the White House to demand the bomb be banned, only to be told by the President that the whole thing was a shuck, there was no bomb. The protesters, left without a raison d'être, reverse themselves and demand the bomb so they can then abolish it. In his own prophetic way, Lenny foresaw what actually did happen when the test-ban treaty was signed: the peace movement, having felt its purpose accomplished, began to disintegrate. A like crisis must have gripped the bureaucrats of the March of Dimes when faced with the development of the Salk and Sabin vaccines. (What do we do now? Muscular dystrophy or birth defects?)

A similar, though rather curious, dilemma periodically bogs down what has come to be known as the peace movement. It is curious because the Vietnam war continues, as atrocious as ever. Bombing has for the moment stopped north of the 17th parallel. Yet it maintains its genocidal level in the South, and in Laos, where half the population has already been forced into a cave existence, bombing missions have been tripled, according to Pentagon releases. Washington—against world popular opinion, at least seven-eighths of the Vietnamese people, and even a majority in this Home of the Brave—continues to represent the Thieu-Ky clique as the legitimate representative of the South Vietnamese. And the Nixon administration, press testimonials to its moderation and flexibility to the contrary, appears no more prepared than its predecessor to remove the half-million occupying forces. The status of the war is much the same, then, as it was five years ago at the time of the Tonkin hoax. The only added ingredients are 500,-000 more U.S. troops and, on the "hopeful" side, a few hundred diplomats in Paris and a by-now-consensus opinion that the aggressors can never win the war.

After five years of teach-ins, marches large and small, sit-ins and "mobile tactics," draft refusals, evasions and desertions, electoral campaigns and petitions and advertisements, destruction of draft records and indeed of draft offices, after five years of protest, dissent and resistance, the war continues. And the movement must now be about the serious business of creating the means for a prolonged difficult struggle.

Maxwell Taylor, one of the first architects of U.S. strategy in the war, holds that this is the war to end all wars of national liberation, to prove they don't work. Washington has brought all its power to bear to make that point. It has chosen to make this the epic battle of our time, and we cannot afford to let Vietnam lose, even on minor concessions. *Look* magazine has said, "The Far East is now our Far West." That is, Vietnam is no aberration in an otherwise humane policy; nor is it an ideological binge. It is part of a drive for outward expansion and world hegemony inherent to U.S. capitalism. And if the system is prepared to spend a billion or two on bush wars on poverty at home, it does so to insure domestic peace so as to continue the Vietnams unhampered. But this war has forced to the surface the conflict between military priorities and domestic social needs. Excessive investment in war, with its high profit yield, has distorted the entire economy at the expense of social needs. Seymour Melman has estimated a backlog of social priorities requiring a minimum of $76 billion a year more than what is being spent now. Such a huge sum can only come from corporation profits and armament expenditures. The fight against the war, and the system it represents, is therefore central to all strategic considerations for the movement.

Present movement problems lie not in a poor past strategy, but rather in the lack of any strategy at all. Strategic considerations have never been the forte of the North American left; tactics have always been its peculiar genius, but tactics without strategy have also always resulted in opportunism, co-optation, spontaneity, and frustration. Tactical debates have seemed to dominate antiwar forces throughout the Vietnam war. They have eliminated strategic considerations, and at times rendered the war itself irrelevant. There has been a continual one-sided outlook that has argued, "We tried demonstrations and they didn't work," or "We tried peace candidates and that didn't work." Were the Vietnamese to have held, for example, that, "We tried antiaircraft and that didn't work," the war might well have been over long ago. The first lesson the Vietnamese have taught us is that one leaves no tactics unused that will expand the unity of the national struggle. The responsibility for stopping this Vietnam and future "Vietnams" falls heavily on the backs of antiwar forces in our country, and our best contribution toward meeting that responsibility is to build the strongest movement for confronting the authority, to tie down the enemy at home.

It is becoming increasingly clear that the problems confronting the nation will not be solved by liberal answers, even those with the best of intentions. In New York City, over a million people now live, after a fashion, on welfare. The well-meaning liberal urban coalition cannot meet that horror any better than five dollars a day and carfare home can solve urban unemployment. In that city, the world capital of finance, only a thorough overthrow of the present relationship of institutions, one that takes money from the banks and insurance companies and gives it back to the people who earned it, will begin to meet the crisis. In Brecht's *Threepenny Opera*, one character announces that some poor people just held up a bank, and another replies that that's a switch.

Tens of thousands of North Americans, mostly young, both black and white, are coming to see the need for a drastic, that is to say, revolutionary, reordering of national priorities and institutions, and to see this transformation coming about through a cataclysmic forceful process where power is wrested from one set of interests and wielded by another through its own institutions. Marx wrote that the bourgeousie produces its own gravediggers. His saying so doesn't make it so, but his observation is profoundly accurate. It is the wasteful, absurd, exploitative and violent system that runs this country that has produced these new thousands committed to plow it under. It is now a fight of these new revolutionaries to maintain their essential humanity against the old order that deforms and warps.

Bourgeois politics may be the art of the possible, but revolutionary politics must be the development of the potential. When the gap between the demand for an improvement in the quality of life, and the ability of the power structure to meet the demand, becomes intolerable, a revolutionary situation is present. What is necessary, however, is consciousness, the appreciation of those involved in struggle for what it is possible to do in this society, and what is actually being done. If masses of people, for example, come to see the need for a complete demilitarization of society, and this system cannot meet that need, then that is too bad for the system; the need and therefore the demand stands. If this system cannot end racist oppression, and if folks come to understand that an end to such oppression is necessary for their own well-being, well, then, fuck the system. Insofar as reform struggles bring out the question of power in a concrete way, it is possible to build a movement around that question that cannot be easily diverted by illusions that come with the selective concessions that the present order has the capacity to dispense.

When the war in Vietnam is finally over, the impact on the internal life of this country will be terrific. The polarization that is now developing will undoubtedly become more acute. Any concessions the U.S. might win would embolden those who seek to impose a Pax Americana on the world, just as a retreat will stimulate hysteria in those same circles, the cry of dominoes, and "let's go with a winner." The derangements that swept the country in the form of the Palmer raids after World War I, McCarthyism after World War II, the Chinese Revolution and the Korean War, Goldwater's rise and the assassination of Kennedy after the Bay of Pigs—all may seem relatively innocuous by comparison with what may happen after Vietnam. Which underlines the importance of building a movement of the widest dimensions, barring no one desirous of ending the war, and at the same time deepening antiwar feelings into anti-imperialist consciousness and in turn to anticapitalist commitment.

The violence that has characterized this country from its inception permeates to the marrow. Rap Brown's observation that violence is as American as cherry pie is proven on a daily basis in every burg from Tacoma to Tallahassee. Police and vigilante repression has already forced many, rightfully, to defend themselves with arms. Provocation and other acts of police agents seek to turn these arms against each other. Obviously armed insurrection and guerrilla warfare are suicidal without a sea of mass support in which to swim. Our first proposition must be that of the Vietnamese, who hold that politics are everything, that all tactics flow from the politics. But it is utopian to assume that the ancient order that rules today will not resort to violence to resist demands for change. If it is prepared to spend billions and billions of dollars and years and years of atrocities to defeat Vietnam, where it has relatively little economic stake, the odds are far better than even that it will not let its treasure be taken here at home by the peaceful passage of constitutional amendments. The violence it wreaks on the poor of the republic, on people of color in Southern plantations and Northern ghettoes and barrios, on the young who people the campuses, all for demanding little more than minor reforms, serves notice as to what its intentions will be when there is a challenge for real power. And it is a singular pain in the ass to watch the daily wringing of well-meaning hands—at the specter of people beginning to defend themselves—as they tremble with the knowledge that when the crunch comes, they will no longer be allowed the luxury of viewing the struggle with fine impartiality.

More and more of us have come to see, on a world scale as well as on our doorstep, that the main enemy we commonly face is our homegrown imperialism. Whatever the difficulties of its main adversaries, the socialist nations, each is better off today than ever before. The Soviet Union has come through half a century dominated by war and famine to become the second world power; today in China, unlike India, garbage trucks pick no corpses off the streets every morning, and if that nation feeds its population two bowls of rice a day, only, and of course it feeds it more, that is a billion and a half bowls daily, an incredible feat and burden; the German Democratic Republic has had to overcome a history as the most violent racist country in this century; Cuba has proclaimed itself the first free territory of the Americas, closer to the colossus than Philly is to New York; North Korea has become, next to Japan, the most industrialized country in Asia, fifteen years after it was razed to the ground. If there are distortions and immense difficulties in these countries, still they are all more democratic today than they ever were. The problems they face of wealth and development are greatly worsened by the United States and allies of the empire. What is revolutionary about their development is that they seek to change the entire course of human history, to alter thousands of years of man using the labor of other men for profit. To remake society so that power resides in the people, after thousands of years of elites and epic inhumanity, is a task not lightly undertaken and not easily accomplished. Not in ten years. Nor in 50. The *mishegoss* of violence and the ingrained racism in our own country will be legacies any new society constructed here will have to deal with for a long time to come. But that is just what we are about the business of doing; building a United States of America where people come first.

I think the most important conversation I've ever had was with Premier Pham Van Dong in Hanoi. We got to talking about the antiwar movement in this country and at one point the Premier turned to us Americans and said, "You know, we thank you for what you are doing for us. But of course we expect it of you;

that is your responsibility as human beings." He said, "That is our relationship with all our friends around the world—the Soviets, the Chinese, the Latins, the French. We thank you for what you are doing for us. But at the same time you must thank us for what we are doing for you." He was saying that the Vietnamese fight and the democratic movements in our own country are part of a common struggle against a common enemy, that each Vietnamese victory is a victory for all of us, that their final victory will be for all of us. Two days before the interview, we were handed an invitation to the DRV Afro-Asian Solidarity Committee rally "in defense of the American Negroes' struggle against discrimination and police brutality in Watts, Los Angeles." This, while bombs were dropping on their own land.

Premier Pham repeated his words, "We thank you for your help but you must thank us." In fact, he was saying, we are helping defeat your enemy for you. The people who kill us will kill you too; those who own the mines of South Africa also own the fields of California. And when Maxwell Taylor or William Rodgers speaks of losing Vietnam, to whom is he losing? To the Vietnamese. They lost China to the Chinese and Cuba to the Cubans. They are losing Laos to the Laotians, Mozambique to the Mozambicans and Syria to the Syrians. What we must say is that some day they will lose the United States to the people who live and work here. Power to the people.

This book was set on the linotype in Bodoni Book.
The display face is Bodoni Book.
It was set, printed, and bound at H. Wolff Book Manufacturing
Co., New York.
The design is by Jacqueline Schuman.

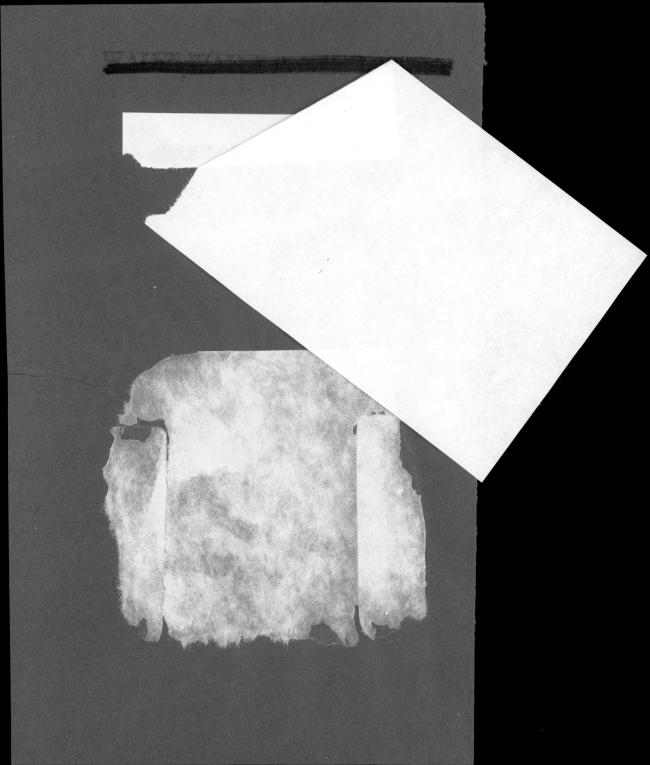